MY FRIENDS' BELIEFS
A Young Reader's Guide to World Religions

also by Hiley H. Ward

Feeling Good About Myself
Religion 2101 A.D.
The Far-out Saints of the Jesus Communes
Rock 2000

My FRIENDS' BELIEFS

A YOUNG READER'S GUIDE
TO WORLD RELIGIONS

HILEY H. WARD

Walker and Company   *New York*

Library of Congress Cataloging-in-Publication Data

Ward, Hiley H.
  My friends' beliefs: a young reader's guide to world religions / by Hiley H. Ward.
    p.   cm.
  Includes index.
  Summary: "Visits" some twenty religious groups around the United States, introducing at each "stop" a young member who shares both his religion's history, beliefs, and practices and his own everyday life.
  ISBN 0-8027-6792-3. ISBN 0-8027-6793-1 (lib. bdg.)
  1. Religions—Juvenile literature. [1. Religions.] I. Title.
BL92.W37 1988   291—dc19   87-29953

Book Design by Laura Ferguson

PHOTO, ART CREDITS:
Hiley Ward: pp. 1, 7, 27, 32, 83, 91, 95, 100, 103, 107, 111, 116, 131, 137, 143.
Religious News Service: pp. 4, 11b, 17, 23, 24, 29, 49, 69, 73, 96, 109, 149, 152.
Westminster Press: pp. 11a, 105, 112, 123, 164. Picture search courtesy of Pat
   Steiner.
Tony Spina (chief photographer, Detroit Free Press): pp. 41, 52.
Max Pelleschi: pp. 67, 77.
Kim Kitamura: pp. 119, 124.
MAPS: Gary Gehman, Don Charles.

Text art (symbols) by David Linn

Printed in the United States of America

10 9 8 7 6 5 4 3 2 1

To my grandchildren,
Mary and Jay

CONTENTS

CKNOWLEDGMENTS

Heartfelt appreciation goes to those who selected and helped to make arrangements for the young persons interviewed in their places of worship across the country. Thanks, too, to the readers of each chapter.

The Jewish Path: Rabbi Marc Tanenbaum, national director, International Relations Department, American Jewish Committee, New York; Connie Reitzes, American Jewish Committee, Kansas City, Mo.; Rabbi Mark H. Levin, Congregation B'nai Jehudah, Kansas City, Mo. *Reader:* Rabbi A. James Rudin, national director, Interreligious Affairs, American Jewish Committee, New York.

The Hindu Path: Kana Mitra, Villanova University, Villanova, Pa. *Reader:* Dr. Pradyumna S. Chauhan, Beaver College, Jenkintown, Pa.

The Buddhist Path: Ven. Mahathera Gunaratana, Buddhist Vihara Society, Washington, D.C. *Readers:* Dr. Guy R. Welbon, professor, religious studies and South Asia regional studies, and chairperson, Department of Religious Studies, University of Pennsylvania, Philadelphia; Scott Wellenbach, scholar-in-residence, Nalanda Translation Committee, Armdale, Nova Scotia, Canada.

The Islamic Path: Imam Mohamad Jawad Chirri, Islamic Center of Detroit; Albert Harp, youth leader, Islamic Center of Detroit. *Reader:* Albert Harp.

The Christian Path—Roman Catholics: The Most Rev. James W. Malone, bishop of Youngstown, Ohio, and former president of the National Conference of Catholic Bishops; Rev. John DeMarinis, pastor, St. Anthony's Roman Catholic Church, Youngstown, Ohio; Sister Joyce Candidi, Oblates Sister of the Sacred Heart, Youngstown, Ohio. *Readers:* Sister Joyce; Rev. Eugene Shaw, S.J., Temple University, Philadelphia, Pa.

Greek Orthodox: His Eminence Archbishop Iakovos, primate of the Greek Orthodox Church of North and South America; Rev. Dr. Robert G. Stephanopoulos, dean, Greek Orthodox Archdiocesan Cathedral of the Holy Trinity, New York, and his wife, Nikki Stephanopoulos, director of news and information, Greek Orthodox Archdiocese of North and South America. *Readers:* Dr. and Mrs. Stephanopoulos.

Episcopalians: Rt. Rev. Peter James Lee, bishop, Diocese of Virginia, Richmond, Va.; Rev. Andrew Kunz, St. Peter's Episcopal Church, Richmond. *Readers:* Glenn Colliver, archivist, Diocese of Pennsylvania, Philadelphia, Pennsylvania; Rev. David Gracie, Episcopal Chaplain, Temple University, Philadelphia.

Lutherans: Dan Cattau, director, News Bureau, Lutheran Council in the U.S.A., New York; Rev. Charles H. Maahs, pastor, Atonement Lutheran Church, Overland Park, Kansas, newly elected bishop of the Missouri-Kansas Synod of the new Evangelical Lutheran Church of America. *Reader:* Dan Cattau.

Presbyterians: Alan Kratz, News Services, Communications Unit, Presbyterian Church in America, New York; Rev. Dr. James Carter, pastor, St. Charles Avenue Presbyterian Church, New Orleans, La. *Readers:* Robert Fles, chairperson, Christian Education Committee, Presbyterian Church of Chestnut Hill, Philadelphia, Pa.; Jean C. Elliott, staff person, General Assembly Nominating Committee, Presbyterian Church (U.S.A.), Philadelphia, Pa.

Methodists: Nelson Price, associate general secretary, Division of Public Media, United Methodist Church, New York; George Conklin, Pacific School of Religion, Berkeley, Calif.; Judith Favor, Berkeley, Calif., who on assignment for this book interviewed the young Methodist, Scott Fujita. *Reader:* Edwin H. Maynard, Dayton, Ohio, former news editor of the national Methodist *Christian Advocate* and assistant general secretary, General Commission on Communications, United Methodist Church.

Baptists: Rev. Dr. Walter B. Pulliam, pastor, Judson Memorial Baptist Church, Minneapolis, and president, American Baptist Churches in the U.S.A. *Reader:* Dr. Pulliam.

Pentecostals: Adon Taft, religion editor, *Miami Herald;* Deborah Alessi, director of administration, Grace Church of Kendall, Miami, Fl. *Reader:* Deborah Alessi.

Thanks also to the administrators and public relations persons who provided information and contacts for the groups and young people mentioned in the final chapter.

Thanks also to my wife, Joan Bastel, who painstakingly read the manuscript and offered helpful advice and to Barbara Bates, editor, whose faith in this book helped to make it possible and who, in her expert guidance, helped to steer this book along to its successful completion.

UTHOR'S NOTE

There are many religious bodies in the world—some three hundred in the United States alone.

This book deals with the major groupings—each with many other groups within them.

The major groups are treated generally chronologically in terms of when they started in history, although most in some way trace themselves to the beginning of time.

In treating the Christian groups, all of which feel they are traceable to Christ, those that have the strongest emphasis on sacraments and order of worship are taken up first and the book moves on to the less formal. The lineup could be reversed; except the approach of moving from formal and "liturgical" churches to the less formal and less ordered churches is close to the way the churches developed in history.

The author regrets that in dealing with the broader strokes or categories not every small group could be included.

In regard to Scripture and holy writing quotations, the Jerusalem Bible is used for the Jewish religion and the King James Version of the Bible for Christians and also standard translations for the other religions. In each case, however, the older English of "thee" and "thou" and "thy" has been changed to "you" and "your," and some verbs have been adjusted accordingly, as well as some punctuation.

NTRODUCTION

Ever wonder why somebody believes or does something that seems strangely different?

Ever wonder how a person becomes a member of another faith?

Ever wonder what John or Mary or Ali or Sarah do at their places of worship and prayer?

Just what is a Jew, Christian, Muslim, Hindu, Buddhist? Just what is a Roman Catholic, Orthodox, Episcopalian, Lutheran, Presbyterian, Methodist, Baptist, Pentecostal?

Come along with us on a journey. . . .

A baby is dipped into water thrce times.

A teenager has his head shaved and in a special rite dons a sacred orange robe.

Another young person takes around his shoulder and chest the sacred thread that he will wear the rest of his life.

Another kneels, sits back, then bends forward to touch his head to the floor in prayer.

Then there are the sounds of strong voices calling the faithful to prayer, the solemn chants, the melodious hymns, the rhythms of resounding scriptures in sacred languages. We hear the joyful speaking in strange tongues of young people filled with the Spirit, and we hear the soaring majestic organ tones in houses of worship.

Come with us in this book to the living religions of your friends and neighbors. Learn about the great leaders of the religions and the beliefs they inspire. Know the deep-felt, holy practices of your friends. Understanding their faith will help you to better understand your own, as you see how they are different and also how much they may have in common.

MY FRIENDS' BELIEFS
A Young Reader's Guide to World Religions

THE JEWISH PATH

Leslie Hellman beside the menorah in the temple of the Congregation B'nai Jehudah, in Kansas City, Missouri.

The Lord is my shepherd; I shall not want.

He makes me to lie down in green pastures; he leads me beside the still waters.

He restores my soul: he leads me in the paths of righteousness for his name's sake.

Yea, though I walk through the valley of the shadow of death, I will fear no evil: for you are with me; your rod and your staff they comfort me.

You prepare a table before me in the presence of my enemies: you anoint my head with oil; my cup runs over.

Surely goodness and mercy shall follow me all the days of my life: and I will dwell in the house of the Lord forever.

—Psalm 23, a Psalm of David

BRAHAM: FATHER OF A NATION

The Jewish religion is the story of one wonderful, almighty Being who made the worlds and the heavens. He is so great that most Jews do not dare pronounce or write his name in full. That is why God is spelled "G-d." In the Hebrew language, the highest name is "Yahweh." When a Jewish leader reads the Hebrew Scripture, he will not read the sacred name Yahweh, but in its place he will say "Adonai," which means Lord because God's name is so sacred.

The Jewish religion is also the story of a people of God, often called the Chosen People. The Jewish people were called especially by God to help make his will known on earth. This was not an easy task, for God gave many rules for his faithful to follow. These rules were aimed at helping to make a person better and more willing to listen to God and his will. These rules also promised to make the world a better place in which to live.

When God decided to choose a people, he also chose one man to help bring them together. God called the man "Abraham," which means "the father of a people or nation." Abraham came from far away to the eastern end of the Mediterranean Sea, to a land known in much of history as Canaan, or Israel. His descendants formed the nation of ancient Israel. Over the centuries, this land fell to many conquerors from all directions.

Through the centuries, Jews continued to believe in the idea of a chosen people and a chosen land. In 1948, the state of Israel was formed, largely the area of the ancient land of Israel. Many Jews believe this fulfills a promise of God to provide a nation for his people today. Yet others, namely Arabs, also believe that they too have a right to a part of the area as a homeland.

Abraham lived at first in Ur of the Chaldees in Babylon. Today Ur would be in Iraq near the Iran border. Ur was only a dozen miles, by some accounts, from the original Garden of Eden. According to Scripture, this is where the first man and woman, Adam and Eve, lived, and from where they were sent after they disobeyed God. (Adam had eaten the forbidden fruit offered by Eve.)

Abraham's family moved north from Ur to the land of Haran, today a part of Turkey, which was a land of idol worshippers. But Abraham worshipped only one God.

Abraham was already about seventy-five years old in about 2,000 B.C.*, when God told him: "Get you out of your country, and from your kindred, and from your father's house, unto a land that I will show you; and I will make of you a great nation, and I will bless

---

*Jews say B.C.E., *"Before the Common Era."*

you, and make your name great; and you shall be a blessing. And I will bless them that bless you. . . ."*

Abraham traveled with his wife Sarah and others over hundreds of miles of rocky terrain. They passed through Egypt, far to the south, then turned north. Abraham had a small fighting force with his caravan, three hundred or so armed men, and he conquered some wicked tribal kings. The cities of Sodom and Gomorrah had become so wicked that God himself destroyed them with fire and brimstone.

Abraham was a good-hearted man, and one story tells how he kindly gave food and lodging to three visitors. They turned out to be angels.

Abraham and Sarah became very old, but God miraculously gave them a son, Isaac, in their old age. In order to test Abraham, God ordered him to kill Isaac on an altar as a sacrifice. In faith, Abraham prepared to do so. As Abraham raised the knife, an angel of the Lord stayed his arm, and the boy Isaac was saved. The angel praised Abraham for being willing to trust God so much.

Isaac grew up and had twin sons, Jacob and Esau. It was Jacob who became important in Jewish history, for he had twelve sons who were the founders of the twelve tribes of Israel.

AN IMPORTANT LEADER

MOSES: HE SAVED HIS PEOPLE

The story of Moses, one of the best known and one of the most important of the Jewish leaders, begins with Joseph, a great-grandson of Abraham. Joseph was a very special boy. He was younger than his brothers and spoiled by his father, Jacob. Joseph had a splendid coat of many colors, and it made him very happy. But the brothers were dressed plainly. As they went about tending their sheep on the mountain slopes, they were jealous of Joseph; so jealous that the brothers seized Joseph and sold him into slavery to a caravan bound for Egypt.

Joseph was able to help the king of Egypt, Pharaoh, understand his dreams, and for that he was given high office. Then one day, the brothers who had treated Joseph so badly arrived to plead for grain to keep their families far to the north from starving.

---

*From *The Hebrew Bible With English Translation* (Jerusalem, 1953) Genesis 12: 1–3. Jerusalem Bible Publishing Company.

Joseph learned that now there was a younger brother, Benjamin. Joseph told his brothers he would not help until they returned with the younger brother. Upon the return of all of the brothers, there was a happy reunion.

But as the years went by, the descendants of Joseph and his brothers who remained in Egypt were taken into slavery.

Moses was born during the time of slavery. His mother, fearing that the baby Moses would be killed, put him in a basket and set him adrift on the water. But Moses was found, adopted by Pharaoh's daughter, and raised in kingly splendor. However, his real mother was taken on as a nursemaid, and she taught Moses about his Jewish heritage.

Moses bringing the Ten Commandments down from Mount Sinai. By Gustave Doré.

4

When Moses became a man, God spoke to him through a burning bush. Moses learned he was to lead his people out of their slavery and suffering to a Promised Land, the land of Canaan, in the area of today's Israel.

But the evil Pharaoh would not let the Jewish people go. God sent ten plagues of disease, destruction, and death on the Egyptian people until the Jews were freed. The Red Sea opened to let the Jews across. The Pharaoh's men followed. When the Egyptian troops entered the path in the water, they were swallowed by the waves.

For forty years, Moses and the children of Israel wandered in the desert. Before they reached the Promised Land, Moses climbed Mt. Sinai to pray. God gave Moses Ten Commandments to take to his people. The Commandments are, in brief:

> You shall have no other gods before me.
> You shall not worship any graven image.
> You shall not take the name of the Lord your God in vain.
> Remember the Sabbath Day, to keep it holy.
> Honor your father and your mother.
> You shall not kill.
> You shall not commit adultery.
> You shall not steal.
> You shall not bear false witness.
> You shall not covet anything that is your neighbor's.

God took care of Moses and the wanderers in the desert. One time God sent a kind of bread, manna, down from heaven to feed them.

The Jews built a tentlike place of worship, a tabernacle with a sacred area that included the ark, an ornate chest. The ark contained the stones on which the sacred commandments were written.

Moses was not allowed to enter the Promised Land, but God led him to a mountain where he could see it. Then Moses died, and it is said in Scripture that God himself buried Moses in an unmarked place. Joshua, who was trained by Moses, led the people into the Promised Land.

The Jews have often been a persecuted people. One of the most terrible persecutions occurred in the modern era when Adolf Hitler, as leader of Nazi Germany, sought to kill all the Jews in Germany and in the lands he conquered. This attempt at genocide—the killing of a whole nation or people—has become known as the Holocaust, a name for total destruction as if by fire. The Holocaust, claiming over six million Jews, many of them gassed and burned in concentration camps, is remembered often in Jewish prayers and ceremonies.

Very important in Judaism also are the prophets—holy men of God who had a way with God's help of finding out the sins of the time and calling the king and nation to change their ways. They also had visions of new days, and some told of a coming messiah, a God-sent leader for Israel. Especially were the prophets concerned with bringing social justice. A number of the books of the Hebrew Scriptures and the Old Testament are named after the prophets. Some of the bigger books of Scripture by prophets are Isaiah, Jeremiah, and Ezekiel.

B EING A JEW

The name "Jew" comes from "Judah," the name of a great-grandson of Abraham. Judah became the name of one of the twelve tribes of Israel, and the name for the southern kingdom, with Jerusalem as its capital.

Because there are different groups in Judaism today, there are some differences of opinions as to who is a true Jew. Basically, a Jew is one who is born of Jewish parents. There are also people who convert to Judaism.

There are two main rituals for becoming part of the Jewish religion: (1) a ceremony shortly after birth, at which time names are given, and (2) an initiation rite into adulthood and into the responsibilities of the Jewish community.

The first ceremony comes eight days after birth for boys. It involves a physical rite, circumcision, or "Brit Milah" as it is called in Hebrew. It is a surgical procedure on the male organ. Indeed, many boys of all faiths and backgrounds in many parts of the world are circumcised.

In the Hebrew Bible, or Old Testament of the Christian Bible, circumcision is a sign of the agreement between God and his people. A boy is usually given a name during the ritual of circumcision. A girl is usually given her name in the synagogue, or place of worship, on the Sabbath or day of rest, Saturday, after her birth.

Bar Mitzvah, "son of the commandment," and Bat Mitzvah, "daughter of the commandment," are ceremonies held traditionally at the age of thirteen. The age thirteen corresponds to the initiation age among many peoples and other religions. Native American and African tribes hold ceremonies introducing youngsters to adulthood between the ages of twelve and fourteen. Some Christian groups use the term "confirmation" for a ceremony at this age period.

EET A BAT MITZVAH

One recent Bat Mitzvah is Leslie Hellman, aged thirteen, of Kansas City, Missouri. Her Bat Mitzvah was one of the big moments of her life—and indeed her parents thought so, too. According to her father, a physician, the occasion was so important that it drew relatives and friends from several states to the ceremony at Congregation B'nai Jehudah in Kansas City, Missouri.

In a Bar or Bat Mitzvah ceremony, the young person has a lot to do, perhaps more than in any initiation rite in other religions. Leslie had a head start, because from the beginning she had attended school at the Hebrew Academy, where the boys and girls must learn Hebrew and other important aspects of the Jewish religion.

Much of a Bar or Bat Mitzvah ceremony consists of demonstrating that the new adult-to-be member of the congregation can read and understand Hebrew. Leslie wanted her Bat Mitzvah to be a "challenge," she said, so she prepared to do more, at least to read more Scripture in Hebrew than was required.

Leslie was expected to conduct the entire religious service on the Sabbath. Bar and Bat Mitzvahs can also be held on several other days of the week, but they often fall on the Sabbath, Saturday. Leslie's temple had quite a few such ceremonies. "If we had more Bar and Bat Mitzvahs," she said, "I don't know when the rabbis would conduct sabbath services!"

Jews often describe the ceremony as "going up" to the Torah.

The Torah consists of the first five books of the Hebrew Bible. The books, written by Moses—who brought the Ten Commandments down from the presence of God on Mount Sinai—are regarded as "the teaching." The books are sometimes referred to by others as the books of law, because these books consist not only of history but of many laws and regulations.

Leslie conducted her Bat Mitzvah ceremony at a pulpit, or lectern. Behind her was a backdrop of scrolls—ancient copies of "the teaching" handwritten on sheepskin. She read in Hebrew from the Book of Numbers, and then she read a "conclusion," or Haftarah, from Hosea, one of the books of the prophets. A cantor (a person who helps with the worship, especially the chanting and singing) stood next to her. His job was to read along silently with Leslie so he could help if necessary.

Early in her Bat Mitzvah ceremony, facing a sea of parents, friends, and congregation members from the "bimah" or platform, Leslie read slowly but strongly a required "personal statement," or prayer: "In this world there are people suffering—suffering because of unreasonable hate, or prejudice. We can hurt our fellow humans by hating or mistrusting them simply because of their coloring, religion, nationality, or in countless other ways.

"I know I have been guilty of this by ignoring someone just because what they were wearing didn't match, or I didn't like their hair style, or in various other silly ways, instead of getting to know the person and finding out what they were really like inside.

"G-d, help me to understand that every human is equal and should be treated fairly, so I can help make the world a better place for everyone. AMEN."

Leslie then directed the people to readings of prayers and blessings in a book they all had before them, *The New Union Prayer Book*. She also read translations of her Hebrew Scripture readings.

She ended the ceremony by reading a four-page typed speech that was to include some of her "deep thinking" about Bat Mitzvah.

Since Leslie likes stories, she decided to start the closing speech with a story. She used to enjoy stories her dad told her when she was younger—stories from a make-believe "Book of Tuna," fish stories that really sounded very true. Then she told of a book she had read, *Anna to the Infinite Power*. Anna at the start of the book is selfish, but she learns to reach out to her brother and help him. "She changed and became more herself. I tried to think of ways this applied to me—and I came up with so many ideas I could hardly believe it!"

Now officially a part of the congregation and the adult Jewish community, Leslie, like Anna, has responsibilities to others.

Some of the things she is doing to help others include working with the younger children at the Hebrew Academy. Of course, she enjoys telling them stories about "funny creatures with purple eyes and green noses."

And she has other ideas about how she might serve and be a "blessing" to others.

"As an adult member of the Jewish community," she also explained in her Bat Mitzvah speech, "I feel that I should reach out and try to help everyone. My first step will be to contribute ten percent of my Bat Mitzvah money for *tzedakah*. I know it is only a little step, but it is a step forward." *Tzedakah* is a name for a "charity" box found in Jewish synagogues and homes where a person can put money to help people in need.

Leslie continued: "Another way I will try to help is illustrated in my Torah portion. In it, G-d commands us not to cut off the family of the Kehathites [an ancient group] from the midst of the Levites [a priestly group]. If we all work at not cutting off people in our midst just because they are different, I know the world will be a better place for everyone."

B RANCHES OF JUDAISM

In North America, the three main branches of Judaism are Orthodox, Reform, and Conservative.

The Orthodox Jews are the strictest. They separate men and women at the services, follow strict *kosher* dietary, or food, laws—no pork or crawling seafood; no mixing of milk and meat products, among other laws. They use head coverings such as the *yarmulke*, or skull cap, and they use the *tallis*, or prayer shawl, and the *tefillin*—small leather containers containing Scripture quotations that are strapped to arms and head. Sabbath rest requires restriction of activities allowed on that day. Orthodox Judaism may also pay more attention than other branches of Judaism to writings and commentaries such as the Talmud, a collection of Jewish civil and religious law. Orthodox Jews believe that a personal messiah, or leader, will come to bring peace to the world.

Reform Judaism is the most liberal and seeks to adapt traditional ways to modern times. Reform Judaism holds the Torah (the Old Testament books of law) as authoritative, as do other branches of Judaism.

Reform Judaism does not believe, by and large, in the coming of a personal leader, but rather in the coming of a messianic age, or period of time in which the will of God will rule.

Conservative Judaism is somewhere between Reform and Orthodox. Leslie's temple is Reform, but her school is Conservative. Like the Orthodox, Conservative Jews keep dietary laws and emphasize Hebrew. Like the Reform, they favor the families sitting together in the services and seek to interpret ancient laws for modern life and education.

THINGS TO KNOW

HOLY DAYS

Chanukah—Also spelled *Hannukah* or *Hanuka*, a "festival of lights" in December, commemorating the defeat of Syrian Greeks by the Maccabees in 165 B.C.E. and the rededication of the Temple in Jerusalem. Miraculously, a tiny container of oil found in the Temple burned for eight days. In celebrating this festival, an eight-branch candlestick, or *menorah*, is used, plus a ninth, or *shammash*, candle used for lighting each of the other candles, one for each day of Chanukah. Children receive gifts and play a top-spinning game.

Passover—A spring festival lasting seven or eight days, recalling the angel of death "passing over" the Hebrews, as the firstborn of the Egyptians were taken by death in the last of the great plagues brought by God on the Egyptian captors. A home and synagogue ceremonial meal recalls the bitter experience of slavery in Egypt and the haste of the escape, or "Exodus." The meal is referred to as the "Seder," which means a precise "order" of items. It includes unleavened bread (there was no time for the escaping Israelites to prepare leavened bread), bitter herbs, eggs, lamb, and wine, each food having a historic symbolism.

Rosh Hashanah—Literally the "head of the year," the Jewish new year, ushering in a period of high holy days for reflection and repentance. A ram's horn, or shofar, is sounded. (A ram was sacrificed by Abraham in place of Isaac.)

Sabbath—A day of rest each week—the seventh and last day of the week—commemorating God's resting on the seventh day of Creation. The observance, a reminder of God's justice and rule on earth, is ordered in the Ten Commandments.

Shavuoth—A "feast of weeks" in the spring that celebrates the giving of the law, or Torah.

Sukkoth—"Feast of booths," a fall harvest festival, marked by putting up harvest booths.

Yom Kippur—"Day of Atonement," the most important holy day, the last of the high holy days. It is a time of confessing of sins, atoning or making amends for wrongdoing, and seeking forgiveness, and it comes ten days after Rosh Hashanah. The shofar, or ram's horn, is sounded at the end of Yom Kippur.

Left: A traditional table setting for the Passover Seder meal. On the center plate is a roasted lamb bone, in memory of the lamb sacrificed at the Temple, and bitter herbs, a reminder of bitter slavery and other symbols. The wafers of matzoh, or unleavened bread, represent the food that the Jews ate in fleeing from Egypt. Right: Blowing the Shofar, or ram's horn, a call to worship in Jerusalem.

SYMBOLS

Menorah—See *Chanukah* above.

Mezuzah—Metal, plastic, or wooden container holding Scripture quotations; they are put on doors or gates following instructions in Deut. 6 : 9.

Scrolls—Ancient people wrote on scrolls. In a Jewish synagogue, or temple, the scrolls are the books of the Torah (the first five books of the Hebrew Scriptures and the Bible). The scrolls are often written on parchment, or sheepskin. Hebrew writing is from right to left, instead of left to right as in English.

Star of David—A six-point star, used on his shield by King David, who wrote many of the Psalms in the Bible.

THE HINDU PATH

Kaustuv Banerjee takes up a crude walking stick broken from a tree, token of the life of a hermit and part of the sacred thread ceremony.

"From the unreal lead me to the real, from the darkness lead me to the light, from death lead me to immortality."

—from a sacred Hindu writing, *Brihad-aranyaka Upanishad*

There are no strong personalities or great leaders that stand out at the beginning of Hinduism. In fact, it is hard to pinpoint in any way how or exactly where Hinduism started. Although Hinduism is concentrated largely in one country, India, it didn't all begin there.

Over three thousand years ago, there were no nations such as there are today. Many people belonged to tribes. There was a strong great tribe called Arya, which moved about Europe and parts of Asia. The Aryans conquered people wherever they went.

Some Aryans settled in Italy, others in Greece, still others in Spain, England, and Persia. Then a group wandered over a range of mountains in central Asia. They settled in the lush Valley of the Indus, which is Pakistan today, north of India.

These Aryans worshipped a "sky father." Offshoot groups in Italy called him Jupiter; the Greeks called him Zeus. Those who settled east of the Indus River, which flows south into the Arabian Sea, developed a group of gods. These people were called Hindus—persons "from the land of Indus." The gods of the Valley of the Indus were not as distinct as those in Greek and Roman history. To the Hindus there is one spirit or force above and beyond all others. He is Brahman, a supreme presence and spirit of the universe. Souls go through many lives, eventually reaching perfection. Then they arc set free to live on a higher plane, Moksha.

The newcomers to the Valley of the Indus created the world's oldest writings. Some say these scriptures are as much as ten thousand years old. The people who settled in the valley developed a language called Sanskrit, now the sacred language of Hindu writings and rituals.

The sacred writings were the *Vedas*. The oldest and most familiar of the Vedas is the *Rig-Veda*, which says that there are thirty-three gods. The gods are all a part of the spirit source, Brahman. Most important of the gods is the mystical creator, Brahma. Next is Vishnu, who assumes many shapes and personalities as he comes to earth to protect and help mankind. Then there is Shiva, a gloomy god of battlefields and death, often pictured as wearing a wreath of skulls. He is also god of dance and fertility. The wife of Shiva is Parvati, "daughter of the mountains," or Uma, "light."

Durga is the goddess who was created by all the gods when a tyranny of demons on earth became unbearable. She is called "shakti," meaning "energy," because she came into being when each god gave a part of his energy to create a goddess. There are other forms of the warrior goddess Durga or Kali. Her other personalities are Annapurna, "the provider of corn," and Saraswati, "the goddess of learning."

MEET A LAD OF THE SACRED THREAD

For much of the day, Kaustuv Banerjee has been a king, or at least the son of a king.

He stands in a long silk maroon royal robe in the center of an imaginary square formed by four potted banana trees. He wears a tapered ornate paper crown that looks rather like a stocking cap. Expensive gold strands are woven into his sleeves. A garland of flowers hangs around his neck.

Kaustuv is not in a castle in old Bengal, India, where his ancestors come from. He is in a rented hall off a busy highway in Audubon, near Philadelphia, Pennsylvania.

The ceremony is the coming of age and dedication rite of the Hindus. Today Kaustuv is to receive the sacred thread that he will wear the rest of his life.

He is to become a Brahmin (or Brahmana), a member of a devoted priestly caste. Brahmin means "one who has God," one who worships and follows Brahman.

In the first part of the ritual, Kaustuv's mother, grandmother, and other women relatives, each dressed in a single beautiful draped cloth, or sari, move around the square formed by the potted trees where Kaustuv stands.

The women, representing childbearing and the ongoing of life, circle the area seven times, praying and chanting.

Kaustuv's mother carries a ceremonial cup of oil that burns softly on its surface. She stops and faces her son. She places the palm of her hand over the flame, then touches gently the head, heart, and right hand of her son with the palm of her hand,

VISHNU: FOREMOST OF THE AVATARS

Some believe that Vishnu actually lived as a person, but most Hindus say Vishnu is a god who has appeared on earth on occasion in different forms. The appearances of gods on earth are called "avatars."

The idea of avatar is most commonly associated with Vishnu. The powerful god Vishnu is sometimes regarded as a second member of a Trinity that includes Brahma, Vishnu, and Shiva. Like Jesus, the second member of the Christian Trinity of Father, Son, and Holy Spirit, Vishnu is made flesh to dwell on earth and accomplish a purpose. But unlike Jesus, Vishnu comes in different forms.

Tradition has it that there have been and will be ten avatars linked with Vishnu. First, Vishnu came as a giant fish to warn mankind of the danger of a flood, and during a great flood on the earth, he pulled the boat of a primitive man to shore. He was also a crocodile that stirred the waters. As a boar, Vishnu hoisted the earth out from among the waters. He was a lion-man, then a dwarf working to block the evil plans of two great demons. As Rama-with-an-axe, a human, he defeated dominating warrior rulers.

The seventh avatar was Rama-chandra, a king's son, sometimes referred to as just Rama, heir to the throne. But his father had made a promise to his second wife that he would grant her one wish. She wanted her own son to be named the next king and she wanted Rama to be banished for fourteen years.

Rama refused to let his father break his promise, but he did agree to a compromise. Rama would let the other son rule while he was in exile. Rama then entered a forest with his wife, Sita, and his brother. He fought and won a war against demons. However, Ravana, ruler of the demons, kidnapped Sita and took her to his kingdom, Lanka, today's Sri Lanka.

Rama joined forces with Hanuman, the monkey king, and they built a bridge of rocks to the island of Ceylon. After a series of battles, Rama rescued his queen. He returned to his kingdom and reigned, it is said, for ten thousand years.

The eighth appearance of Vishnu is Krishna. Hindus regard Krishna as the most important avatar. To some he is the full incarnation or expression of Vishnu.

Krishna on earth was the nephew of an evil king. It was predicted that one of the nephews would kill the king. To be safe, the evil king ordered all his nephews killed. Krishna was taken by his father to the cowherd Nanda, who raised him as his own son.

The boy grew up killing demons in the forest. After that, Krishna returned and killed the wicked king and took over his kingdom. But he was restless and went back to fighting demons in the forest. But one of his followers, mistaking him for a deer, shot and killed him with an arrow.

The ninth avatar is believed by many to be the Buddha, about whom we will learn in the next chapter. The tenth and last avatar still to come is Kalkin. Like the other avatars, he will, by his own birth, suffering, and death, show that the gods and God or God-force are interested in mankind. Kalkin will be a symbol of concern for others, an inspiration to devotion and a source of courage.

AN IMPORTANT LEADER

GANDHI: THE PEACEFUL MAN WHO FREED INDIA

One of the most famous and beloved men of the twentieth century was Mohandas Karamchand Gandhi (1869–1948). A Hindu, he was a man dedicated to peace. He used peaceful demonstrations and marches to force the British to give independence to India, which they had taken over. Independence was won in 1947.

Born in India in a warrior caste family, Gandhi studied law in England, then went to South Africa to work with an Indian law firm. In South Africa, he saw that Indian workers were treated almost like slaves. During the Boer War (1899–1902) in which England defeated the Dutch colonists (Boers) in South Africa, he worked in the Indian Ambulance Corps. Afterward, he bought a farm and tried to live as simply as possible. But in 1906, the government of Transvaal, a province of the Union of South Africa, passed a law requiring all Indians to be fingerprinted. Gandhi called on his people to resist. He led peaceful demonstrations and he was jailed for a while, but the law was repealed in 1914.

Gandhi then turned his sights toward India. After the British massacred a crowd in 1919 in northern India, he dedicated his life to the cause of freedom in India.

He coined the term "satyagraha" which means "true insistence" or "spiritual resistance" and refers to the idea that truth and spirit are enough to win a cause without violence.

Another watchword of Gandhi's was "ahimsa," which means "nonviolence." He took hordes of the population in India to the streets in protest. Again he was jailed. But eventually the British gave in and agreed to independence.

Gandhi was respected by Christians and Hindus alike. He was especially fond of the teaching of Jesus in the Sermon on the Mount as related in Matthew 5, 6, and 7 in the Christian Bible. Many called Gandhi "Mahatma," which means a wise and holy person with special powers. But Gandhi still had enemies. In 1948, he was assassinated by a fanatic who blamed him for the partition between India and Pakistan.

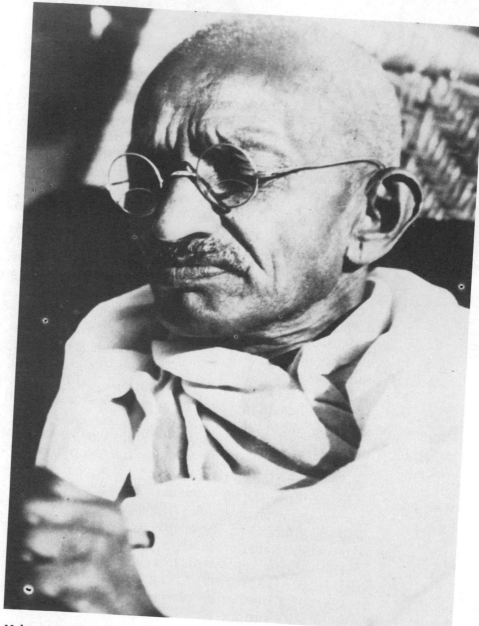

Mahatma Gandhi inspired not only Hindus, but people of all faiths with his simple spiritual life and his dedication to freedom.

"passing" on an eternal flame of knowledge and spiritual blessing. She tells him that the blessing will give him strength and vigor.

Kaustuv's mother repeats her welcome three times and then declares that he is officially a prince. She says that material goods and fine things will be lavished on him.

Then, suddenly, Kaustuv changes his mind, as he must. Kaustuv gives up being a king. The main part of the "sacred thread" ceremony, or "poithe," is about to begin.

The tradition requires that a holy guru, or teacher, be present and conduct the ceremony. But gurus, learned spiritual men who have set themselves off from the usual pursuits of life, are not easily found in the United States. The Hindu faith is not so common here, and life moves at a more materialistic and faster pace.

But it's all right for Kaustuv's grandfather to take the place of the guru in the ceremony. And the grandfather, Ranagit Chatterjee, sits in a white garment, ready for the approach of the initiate.

The young "prince," as Kaustuv has pretended to be, now must say that he is fed up with riches and material possessions. He prefers a life of simplicity, faith, knowledge, and poverty. He is not content to be rich when the world is full of so many poor.

He tells his mother in the ritual, "Mother, I don't want to live in a castle or house. I want to go to my guru."

She begs him to stay, but Kaustuv, in the ceremony, insists that he is called to go out among the people and live simply with thoughts of God.

So he takes off the outer royal robe, which leaves a plain saffron garment. He takes up a crude walking stick broken from a tree, symbolic of the life of a hermit who lives on the hills and as a beggar.

The grandfather tells him, "You will be with me. . . . Follow me and what I say. . . ."

The grandfather burns some straw that he is holding. This symbolizes the perishableness of material goods.

The grandfather brings forth seven strands of sturdy gray "thread," looking very much like ordinary string. Kaustuv moves forward as the grandfather loops the threads around Kaustuv's neck and over his right shoulder. Like a plain necklace of string, it reaches to his waist.

Kaustuv must now wear this string the rest of his life—at school, on the ball field, at home. Traditionally, the Brahmins never take it off, but much of the practice of Hinduism is left up to the person. Kaustuv says he expects to keep the thread on at all times, except when he is taking a shower or swimming. When he is in his school clothing, the string is under his shirt.

The seven strands of string stand for:

1. Power of speech
2. Memory
3. Intelligence
4. Forgiveness
5. Steadfastness
6. Prosperity
7. Good reputation

Kaustuv's grandfather, in the ceremony, gives him two "mantras," two prayer poems in the sacred Sanskrit language. The first offers worship to Lord Brahma, and the second, written by Kaustuv himself, according to custom, is a prayer for power to control himself. This second prayer is a secret prayer known only to Kaustuv and the god, Lord Brahma.

Both of these mantras give Kaustuv special power and strength, but only if he is holding the sacred thread and saying the mantras at the same time.

In India, at least in the older days, a new Brahmin would go off and live and study with a guru. The important point is to seek after knowledge continually, not for rewards or a high-paying job, but for its own sake.

Kaustuv considers going to Haverford College in Pennsylvania, where he is a freshman, as equivalent to a young man in India studying with a guru.

Concluding the ceremony, Kaustuv sits in a lotus position between the trees, his feet under him. Now, as a beggar instead of a prince or king, he receives alms, or gifts. The guru, his grandfather, offers him fruits and sweets. His mother also feeds him, fruit, milk, and yogurt. Until now he has not eaten all day.

Free of all attachments to family and the world, the young man now begins his own search for knowledge. First, there are supposed to come three days and three nights spent in total darkness, although the amount of time is up to the new initiate. Dark caves, such as hermits and the gurus used to seek, are not easy to find these days, so Kaustuv selects the basement of his house on a hill in the suburb of Lower Providence, Pennsylvania. He stays there in darkness for one day and night.

For one year he decides that he will give up meat—and onions! They excite people, he says. He also will try to eat in silence for a time, another traditional custom. All this helps him to control himself, so he will be able to have power over other things, he says.

Kaustuv now can conduct services. These, unlike services in other religions, are not required and may be very infrequent. He can conduct funerals, at which time other Brahmins are invited, but there must be an odd number rather than an even number of Brahmins present.

Kaustuv will say his mantras daily, usually after a morning shower and before sunrise, "a peaceful time of day."

He may take part in an occasional ritual in the home when the family will sit around him as if he were a guru. In his home, there will be a picture of the gods, who can pray, interceding for a person. There will be a picture of the popular god Krishna. His family will say many mantras to the god Brahma. There will be thanksgiving for food, after which fruits and sweets will be given out.

As Kaustuv goes into the world now, he must select a path or career of service. But, as he says, "All careers are service, so all are open." In tradition, Brahmins do not take political power; so, "aspiring to be President or a politician is probably out!" Yet, in tradition, because kings and political figures are expected to follow the advice of Brahmins, the Brahmins are considered most important.

"Being a Hindu means to me," Kaustuv says, "not being showy, practicing simplicity and action.

"I used to worry about what people thought of me," said the tall good-looking youth with rimmed glasses. "But now I don't. I just want to seek knowledge, take action, and dedicate my life to service and charity."

BRANCHES OF HINDUISM

There are many groups within Hinduism. They are distinguished largely by the gods or avatars of Vishnu to which the faithful give their main devotion, and this often depends on what part of India one comes from. The division may be over the emphasis on Brahma or Vishnu or Shiva. And some may worship Durga. A devotee to Vishnu may worship a particular avatar of Vishnu, such as Krishna or Rama.

The *Sikhs* in northeast India are a distinctive group that has split off, but still consider themselves Hindus. Influenced by the Muslims, they believe in one god and reject the idea of many gods and avatars. They wear turbans, or cloths wrapped around their heads; they also wear sacred undergarments. Sikhs do not cut their hair, and they tie back their beards with a netlike cloth. Warriors by tradition, they carry two-edged daggers.

THINGS TO KNOW

Atman—The innermost being in the heart of man; universal breath and spirit at one with Brahman.

Caste—A class of people to which each Hindu traditionally belongs. Originally there were four castes: (1) *Brahmana*, or Brahmin, made up of priests and scholars; (2) *Kshatriya* or *Rajanya*, soldiers or rulers; (3) *Vaishya*, farmers, merchants, craft workers; (4) *Shudra*, servants and slaves. Those who do not belong to any caste are considered outcastes or untouchables and they do the lowest work of all. The Indian Constitution now outlaws such a grouping and gives equal rights to all as citizens.

In the caste system, a person is supposed to stay in his or her place. In a future life one could perhaps move onward to a higher rank.

The caste system was necessary, says Kaustuv, because it was necessary to divide workers and leaders. All could not be leaders. But the modern world with its travel, and the cutback in farming, has made the caste system difficult to keep up.

Karma—If you do something wrong, it will catch up with you later. Karma means "a man is the creator of his own fate" and everything he does will catch up with him.

Pilgrimages—Among the holiest places visited are the seven rivers. Most important is the Ganges River in northeast India. Pilgrimages are usually during May, June, and July. People bathe and wash in the sacred waters.

Reincarnation—Hindus have a love for the earth and believe a person stays on earth for a very long time. He is reborn into many lives, each time, it is hoped, improving himself and reaching a higher state the next time, depending on his karma. Bad people come back as insects and rats. The soul never dies. An aim is to become, in a future life, a Brahmin or Brahmana, a member of the upper class. Eventually upon reaching perfection, one enters the final state of *moksha*, which is freedom from the *karmaic* cycle of birth and death and a state of complete peace.

Because a person might come back by reincarnation as another life form, if not as a person, Hindus do not like to kill other animals. Particularly sacred is the cow, which represents the earth and all that is good in creation.

Kaustuv, as a member of a new generation, says he doesn't hold to the exact idea of reincarnation, that you come back as another person or life form. "To me reincarnation is heredity. You receive the traits of your parents and forebears. I am a manifestation, in a way, of the past."

Sacred writings—There are many writings. The oldest are the *Vedas.* There are four *Vedas: Rig-Veda, Sama-Veda, Yajur-Veda,* and *Atharva-Veda.* There are separate notes and commentaries on the *Vedas* divided into three sections: *Samhitas* (prayers and hymns); *Brahmanas* (rituals and commentary on the *Samhitas*); *Upanishads* (philosophy and ideas recorded as if in conversation).

The second group of writings are the *Puranas,* stories in poetical form of gods and goddesses and great heroes.

Ramayana is a long story about Prince Rama; *Mahabharata* tells the story of battles between two rival families that are related. A part of the *Mahabharata* is the famous *Bhagavad-Gita,* a philosophical poem. In it, Prince Arjuna carries on a discussion about the meaning of life with his chariot driver, who turns out to be the Lord Krishna himself.

Manu Smriti, the "code of Manu," sets forth the laws of the caste system and other laws.

A modern Hindu temple in Portland, Oregon.

An ancient Hindu temple in Bangladesh.

Temple—People do not come to temples as a congregation, but worship in the temple by themselves. Each temple usually honors one god or goddess, although there may be included many shrines to other gods and goddesses. Priests wash the images every day and bring food to these representations of gods. Among the lower castes, if one is not able to get to a temple, a cowshed, since the cow is sacred, may substitute as a temple.

Many Hindus also have shrines at home, and those with larger houses might have a special room for worship. Usually one god or goddess is honored, but there may also be other objects of devotion. Kaustuv's grandmother, for instance, also has a picture of Jesus in her worship room.

Yoga—A Sanskrit word related to the English word, "yoke," *yoga* means "discipline." Creatures who are yoked or held by reins must have discipline. Also there is the idea of "being yoked together with others."

Yoga discipline can take many forms—sitting quietly with legs folded as one meditates, which can include saying mantras, a sacred text or refrain, or repeating the sacred word *Om*; breath control; fasting; fixing the mind on a single thought or object for a time; making the mind blank in order to let ideas flow in.

HOLY DAYS

Dashera—This marks Rama's victory over the demon king, Ravana, who was killed by Rama during battle. This festival is held for ten days in the autumn, usually October. The battle with Ravana and his brother and son is reenacted, and on the tenth day, at the end of the "battle," effigies of Ravana and brother and son—filled with mild explosives—are ignited by "Rama" with a flaming arrow.

Diwali—This is a festival of lights in October or November. On this day Rama returned to his kingdom after fourteen years' exile and conquest over Ravana. The people lit their houses to celebrate his victory over evil. That is why it is called the festival of lights.

Holi—The festival celebrates the victory of truth over falsehood. Since Krishna and his cowherds celebrated "holi" with dance and music, this is how people celebrate it today. Both *Holi* and *Diwali* come at the time of harvest, so they also celebrate the reawakening of nature and the bounty it gives people.

SYMBOLS

Om—This is also written as "AUM." Although basically a mystical sound for which there is no translation, some later interpreters see in it the three Sanskrit Vedic letters for Brahma, Vishnu, Shiva. The markings over it stand for the female counterpart of the three gods.

The sacred word "Om" in the ancient Sanskrit language of India is a popular symbol of Hinduism. It is the symbol that is used at the beginning of this section.

THE BUDDHIST PATH

James Martin stands next to a statue of Buddha's cousin in the garden of the Buddhist Vihara Society, Washington, D.C.

"There should not be glorification of one's own sect and denunciation of the sect of others for little or no reason. For all sects are worthy of reverence for one reason or another. Acting thus one helps grow one's own sect and does good to the other's sect. Acting otherwise he belittles his own sect and does ill to the sect of another. He who glorifies his own sect and denounces the sect of another does so because of excessive love for his own sect. And why? Thinking that his own sect may shine brighter. Acting thus, however, he harms his own sect. Harmony is good. Why? That people may listen to the exposition of each other's doctrine. . . .

—from *Rock Edict XII* (etched on rock) of Emperor Asoka of India, third century B.C.

Unlike Hinduism, which has no one special personality in its history, Buddhism, like Christianity, focuses on the teachings of one person. In Buddhism, this person is Siddhartha, who became known as the "Buddha." Siddhartha was a young prince in a small land in what is now Nepal, along India's northern border.

But the good palace life brought Siddhartha little happiness. He gave up his family and his worldly goods and set off, seeking truth until he found peace of mind. After his experience, Siddhartha became known as "the enlightened or awakened one," which is what "Buddha" means.

He noted these three fundamental or obvious truths:

1. *All life is made up of suffering.* When you think about it, no matter how happy we might become, we have to expect suffering in life. Sickness, disappointments, and death are a part of everyone's life.

2. *All life is changing.* We are never the same today as yesterday, or at this moment compared to a moment ago. Everything is subject to change and decay. The tree grows up, forms leaves, and blooms with the seasons, eventually dies and rots. One of Buddha's most famous stories is the tale of a river. He says a river continues to be a river, although it is changing every second. In fact, the change is so complete, that the water that flows between the banks of the river today is not the same water that flowed in the river yesterday, although it may look the same. Eventually, every drop of water in the river is different from before, yet it is the same river.

   So in life we are constantly changing, although we may seem to be the same person.

3. *There is no unchanging soul or self.* Hinduism holds that the *atman*, or soul, seeks to escape the wheel of life and rebirths to return to the creator-source, Brahman, and enter the state of *moksha*. But Buddha said he could find no trace or hint of a pure soul. While he did not deny the idea of a soul or personal ego or a day-by-day self, he could only talk about *anatman* or *anatta*—"no-ego," a "no-soul."

Buddha searched far and wide for evidence of a soul, but decided that humans are made up of five "aggregates." This human grouping includes the body, feelings, perception (the way we see and understand), predispositions (attitudes), and consciousness. All of these change, and so everything about us, even anything that might resemble a soul or spirit, is always changing. We are more like a changing river than a solid body or person or soul.

The Buddhist, reaching the final destination, Nirvana, which Buddha never really defined, is a living group of aggregates. This takes the place of an individual soul. And Nirvana is not just an after-death attainment. That the Buddha was the Buddha means that he attained Nirvana—and long before his death. To be "awakened" is to attain Nirvana, and such attainment is not limited to after death.

When a person reaches enlightenment and is ready to be absorbed into Nirvana, he or she may elect to renounce Nirvana in order to help others on their way there. Such an *arhat* or *bodhisattva* serves as a sort of saint in a religion that does not include gods as such. The *bodhisattva* does go on to rebirth, in a sense. It is just that he is freed or somewhat freed from the winds of *Karma* that blow us hither and thither when we are reborn.

Buddhism emphasizes the mind and the importance of mind over body. Like Hindus, Buddhists believe in *karma*, which means "works" or "actions," and actions have consequence. What we do in this life will influence who and what we are in the next life. But instead of the next life following from previous events, Buddhists believe that what happens follows more from previous attitudes and thoughts. Physical acts are merely the results of what one wills. So the mind is very important. While others might emphasize rigorous body discipline to purify a person, Buddhists feel that the mind and its thoughts can influence what happens next in this life and the next.

Gigantic Buddha located in Thailand's 700-year-old royal capital, Sukhothai.

Because of the importance of the mind, some kinds of Buddhism allow for mind control over the natural. Some reportedly have been able to see long distances, hear sounds far away, look back into and remember past existences, know other people's thoughts, and even attain special powers of moving through the air, or "levitation." As he meditated under the Bo tree, Buddha "saw" his past existence. There is a story of a follower of Buddha walking on water, as Jesus reportedly did at a later time.

Buddhism, which argues that the caste system is not important, seeks to draw its monks and leaders from all social classes.

SHINING TEACHER LIGHTS THE WAY

Prince Siddhartha, who became the Buddha, was born about 566 B.C. and died about 486 B.C. at age eighty. His family name was Gautama. So he is referred to sometimes as Gautama the Buddha.

His father, who wanted him to take over the kingdom someday, was troubled by fortunetellers who warned that the young prince would eventually leave the kingdom. This would happen, they said, when the prince saw four signs—an old man, a sick man, a corpse, and a beggar.

The king took great care to keep such sights from the eyes of the prince. Yet, while riding from the palace to a garden one day, Siddhartha stumbled on a decrepit old man and wondered about what he saw. Soon Siddhartha came also upon a sick man, a corpse, and a beggar. He decided that all the luxury around him was meaningless.

Siddhartha set out on his quest for peace of mind and happiness. At first, he fasted and lived in the countryside with meager support. Sitting in a stiff position, he plucked out his hair and tormented and tortured his body. He visited various teachers.

But the young prince gained no special insight or spiritual understanding. So he returned to eating and drinking normally. One day as he sat beneath a fig tree, referred to as the *bodhi*, or bo-tree, he meditated and reached deep into his mind. He remembered his past rebirths. He thought hard on the birth and death of other beings according to their deeds in life, and lastly he came to be aware of the need to overcome the things that enslaved his mind—sensual desires, desire for existing, ignorance, and false views. Glowing with wisdom and called by those around him the Buddha, or "enlightened one," he set forth to preach his new wisdom.

He went to the town of Benares, along the Ganges River in north-central India south of Nepal. Here in a deer park at the outskirts of the town, he gave his first sermon.

He explained the four noble truths. They dealt with *dukkha*, a word roughly translated as "suffering." The four noble truths are: (1) life consists of suffering and pain; (2) the origin of suffering and pain comes from craving for or thirsting after sensual and material pleasures; (3) suffering will end when we cease thirsting after or craving pleasure and desires; (4) the conquering of desires and eliminating of *dukkha* can be achieved by following an eightfold path. If one followed this path, he could end his karma, the pattern of continuing rebirth. The eight-step path to overcome craving for pleasure and desire:

1. Right understanding (understanding the four noble truths).
2. Right thought (thinking kindly about other people and various forms of life).
3. Right speech (speaking truthfully and kindly).
4. Right action (acting peacefully, helping others).
5. Right work (earning a livelihood that does not harm others; some regard Buddha as opposed to war.)
6. Right effort (improving one's mind, concentrating on getting rid of unwholesome ideas).
7. Right mindfulness (maintaining awareness and a good state of mind, again, with a concern for others).
8. Right concentration (seeking to awake the mind more). Interestingly, the root word of "buddha,"—"budh,"—means "to wake." Buddhist meditation, with its intense concentration, is aimed at awakening the mind.

BECOMING A TEENAGE MONK

James Martin, fifteen, sat in the middle of the floor in the Washington temple next to a young friend who had come from Singapore in Asia. James, a high school student from Waldorf, Md., put the tips of his fingers together, flattened the palms of his hands as he folded them in silent prayer. Sitting around him, on the floor, were a handful of people, some young, some even gray-haired, looking as distinguished as ambassadors. This house, converted into a Buddhist temple, is about fifteen minutes from downtown Washington, D.C.

Somebody off to the side struck a great gong three times. The Sunday afternoon "vandana" or Buddhist devotional prayers at the Washington Buddhist Vihara were about to begin.

On a wide platform raised two steps from the floor, four monks from Asia in their orange-red robes pulled out cushions. They sat, then bowed, touching their foreheads and folded hands to the floor

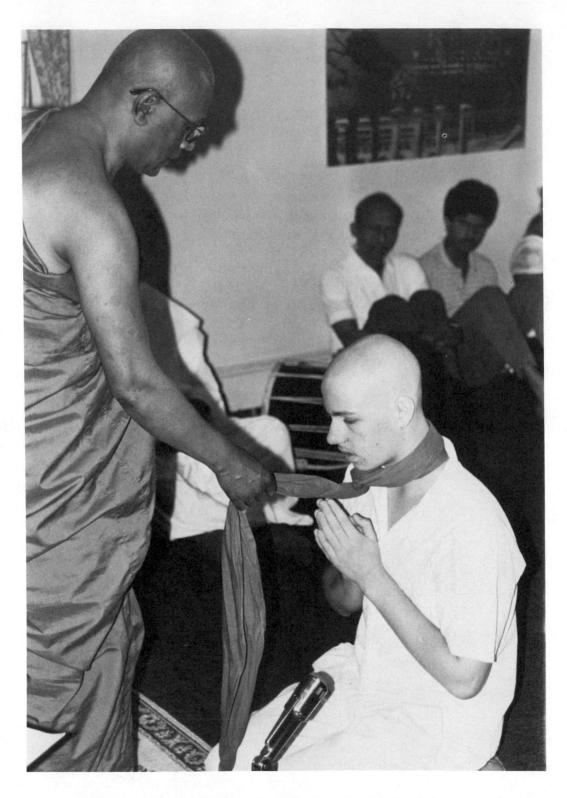

Wrapped in his orange monk's robe, James Martin kneels before the preceptor and asks, "May you forgive all my shortcomings."

before an image of the Buddha about twice life-size. James in his blue-knit turtleneck sweater and light slacks and shoeless like all the others, looked up quietly at the royal brilliance of the Buddha, "the enlightened one."

Four candles sparkled before the Buddha. On each side of the great image were smaller images. Great elephant tusks stood at the far edges. In front was a basket of fruit, a symbol of thanksgiving.

"Sadhu! Sadhu! Sadhu!" the monks said, beginning the ceremony. "Excellent, Excellent, Excellent."

James understands enough of the sacred Pali language to respond in Pali. Together with others in the audience, James joined in words of praise to Buddha:

> Such, indeed, is the Exalted One: worthy, perfectly enlightened, endowed with knowledge and conduct, well-gone, knower of the world, supreme trainer of persons to be tamed, teacher of gods and men, enlightened and exalted. . . .

They recited and pledged to follow the basic eightfold path outlined by Buddha.

The chief monk, the Venerable Mahathera Gunaratana, proceeded to give the sermon from his place on the platform. He talked about *dharma* (Sanskrit) or *dhamma* (Pali) which means "truth" or all that Buddha taught. "He who follows the dhamma, who perfects the dhamma, will be protected by the dhamma," which means that he who follows the truth will be protected by it.

"We can protect the dhamma not by shutting it up but by putting it in daily practice."

There were no offerings taken, but those wishing to contribute could leave money in a large water-cooler jar near the door.

As the worshippers left, they again put on their shoes.

Now, some months later, the scene is still the Washington Buddhist Vihara or temple-monastery. Only, this particular Sunday in early June, James is the main subject of the rite.

The big room on the first floor is packed. After some prayers, James, silent and solemn, dressed in white robes, his head shaved clean as a sign of simplicity and humility, is ushered in. It is the beginning of the ceremony for the ordination of James as a monk. The teenager will be a novice, and for one summer month, he will keep his head shaved and wear the orange robe of the monk. The ceremony is called "pravrajya," or "the going forth." Carrying a folded orange robe, James kneels in the front of the temple room before the leader, or preceptor, Mahathera Gunaratana. James bows three times, his palms and fingers folded together near his fore-head.

He hands over the orange robe to the preceptor, Gunaratana, who sits with six other monks on a raised platform before the brilliant figure of Buddha.

"Venerable Sir, kindly give me ordination," says James in the ancient Pali language. The whole service is in Pali, with English translations in the program. The preceptor takes the robe from James's hands, then gives it back.

James is led out; he returns, now wrapped in the long orange robe of the monks. James kneels again, greets the preceptor and asks, "May you forgive all my shortcomings. May you rejoice in the merits I have acquired. May I rejoice in the merits you have acquired. . . ."

Now James asks the preceptor three times to administer the "refuge" statement. James and the preceptor, Gunaratana, repeat together: "I go to the Buddha for refuge. I go to the dhamma [teaching] for refuge. I go to the Sangha [community of monks] for refuge."

Now James asks for the ten "precepts" or training rules to be said, and James and Gunaratana repeat together in Pali. (Buddhist lay people vow to keep the first five.)

1. "I undertake the training rule to abstain from taking life."
2. "I undertake the training rule to abstain from stealing."
3. "I undertake the training rule to abstain from incelibacy." (That is, he will be celibate, and not marry.)
4. "I undertake the training rule to abstain from false speech."
5. "I undertake the training rule to abstain from intoxicating drugs causing heedlessness."
6. "I undertake the training rule to abstain from eating at improper times."
7. "I undertake the training rule to abstain from dancing, singing, music, and shows."
8. "I undertake the training rule to abstain from wearing gar-lands, using perfumes, and beautifying with cosmetics."
9. "I undertake the training rule to abstain from the use of high and large seats and beds."
10. "I undertake the training rule to abstain from accepting gold and silver."

The congregation and the monks repeat a number of refrains together: "May all calamities be warded off; may all illness be dispelled; may no obstacles hinder me; may I live long and hap-pily."

Ten dhammas, or teachings, that are to be thought of daily by a monk are repeated. They include: "I am now changed into a different mode of life; My life depends on others; I must now behave in a different manner."

Before the ceremony ends, the orange-robed fifteen year old takes his place on the platform with the monks beneath the image of Buddha.

If he decides later to be a full-fledged monk, James, after reaching at least the age of twenty, will be ordained again, this time subscribing to 227 rules. He will be expected to live the life of a monk and be engaged in religious work for the rest of his life, although one can give it up at any time.

After high school, James plans to go to college, majoring in business and psychology. He hopes to go to Thailand, at least for a while. He's already been working for three years on learning the Thai language.

Each day James gets up at 5:00 A.M. and meditates in a half-lotus position, sitting on the floor with one leg folded up over the other. He cups his hands in prayer. Quietly he concentrates, using one of forty breathing exercises.

Learning to concentrate has made a difference with his school work, he says. "Especially in math. . . . I used to be terrible. I'd try hard and spend a lot of time on it, but it wasn't working. Now I'm getting As—in geometry! I can't believe it."

James likes watercolor painting. Occasionally he goes on a movie date. During weekdays, after school, he works for a family, taking care of the house and watching two children.

He doesn't raise his voice, and he enjoys all the learning that comes with the practice of Buddhism. "Everybody's looking for happiness," he says, but he prefers the Buddhist quiet ways. Some founders of world religions, he says, lead you to look out on the world from yourself. "But what sets Buddhism apart," he says, "is that Buddhism looks into how the mind works. It makes you look into yourself."

Some Buddhist groups have created special "rites of passage" for their young people—more secular in tone, but drawn from tradition.

One educator, Scott Wellenbach, a translator of Buddhist documents in a study center in Nova Scotia, Canada, tells of a typical "rite of passage" ceremony he witnessed for thirty young persons in Halifax, Nova Scotia. He refers to one as "Jenny Philips":

Jenny sat between her parents on soft, red cushions in the shrine room. The usual Buddhist shrine is present, but as well there is a special *Shambhala* shrine which has candles, a cup of tea, and offerings of food and other items. *Shambhala* is the tradition, based on Buddhism, that combines the religious teachings of meditation with the concerns of the world, going to work, having a family, and so on, within the vision of living your life decently and honestly and helping to create and maintain a humane and genuine society.

Around Jenny, also accompanied by their parents are many of her friends, boys and girls. Everyone, adults and children, are dressed in their best clothes—some of her friends among the boys are even wearing ties. Jenny has on a blue dress that she received last Christmas ("Children's Day" as these Buddhists refer to it). Lining the walls of the shrine room are some of the adults of the Buddhist community, come to witness this ceremony of transition.

The preceptor of the ceremony, the wife of the Buddhist minister in charge of the center, enters the hall. She is dressed formally and, flanked by her assistants, reminds Jenny of a queen. She lights candles and incense at the shrine, takes her seat, and the ceremony commences.

This traditional Tibetan ceremony of a *lhasang*, a rite of passage, was adapted by western Buddhists, with the guidance of their Tibetan teacher, from Tibetan cultural forms and traditional Buddhist principles. In the *lhasang*, powdered juniper is placed on top of glowing charcoal, so that a juniper smoke arises and wafts through the hall. Though it is a sharp smoke when it comes her way, Jenny notices that she can still easily breathe in the midst of it, unlike the smoke from a wood fire. The *lhasang* is a ceremony of purification, and the smoke represents the burning up and the clearing away of any obstacles to a whole-hearted participation in what is to follow, such as doubts as to what is going on and feelings of wanting the whole thing to be quickly over.

The *lhasang* completed, Jenny's mother and father take her forward to the front of the hall to introduce her to the preceptor. They say hello, shake hands, and then Jenny places on a nearby table a gift that she has brought to the ceremony with her. Jenny was told that the gift was to represent her leaving behind childhood. So she chose a doll that had been very important to her, one that she had received on her last birthday. In a way it was hard to part with it, but it seemed fitting and she did notice that lately she had been playing with it less. As Jenny returns to her seat, her mother and father step to the back of the room. She is left alone in the center, though in the company of her friends.

At this point the sacred clowns enter. They amuse, as any clown will, but also instruct in the principles of earth, water, fire, and air. Most memorable is the earth clown. He says that it is time to give up the daydreams of childhood and to come down to earth, and that is what meditation practice is all about. Jenny doesn't herself meditate, but her parents do and she is interested to learn that coming down to earth is what they are trying to do when they meditate. The clown of earth also teaches how to bow, Japanese style, from a kneeling position with body held close to the ground. He says that bows are to acknowledge mutual respect.

After the clowns leave, Jenny, along with the other young people, goes forward to receive an arrow and a flower from the preceptor. When all are reseated, the preceptor gives a short talk, explaining that the arrow represents fearlessness and the flower, gentleness. At eight years old the children are starting to emerge from their parents' care and are encouraged to rely on fearlessness and gentleness as they begin to explore the world.

They have both a responsibility and a privilege. The responsibility is to start to take care of themselves and not to rely entirely on their parents. The privilege is that they are urged to question and investigate how and why things work as they do. They no longer need accept blindly what they are told.

The rite of passage is now completed. The preceptor leaves the shrine room, and as the children go, they are showered with confetti. The children ask that the gifts that they had offered—the dolls and toys and games—be donated to the children's wing of a local hospital. To celebrate, Jenny and her parents and Jenny's best friend, Sarah, and her mother and father all have a festive dinner together.

B RANCHES OF BUDDHISM

There are two major groupings in Buddhism: Mahayana and Theravada. Buddhists in Northern Asia are primarily associated with the Mahayana school, particularly in Tibet, China, Mongolia, Korea, and Japan. "Mahayana" means "greater vehicle," and so is meant to indicate it will carry more people to Nirvana than other approaches. This group in particular believes that there are many lesser enlightened beings—those who have achieved enlightenment—who can, as *bodhisattvas*, or saints, lead many to Nirvana. Mahayana Buddhists hold Buddha to be almost like a god.

Buddhists in Sri Lanka, Burma, Vietnam, Laos, and Cambodia are likely to be of the Theravada school. The name means "the way of the elders." The school has been called the *Hinayana* school—meaning "lesser vehicle." This name was given it somewhat in mockery by the Mahayanas, so the Theravadas do not like to use it. A Theravada is more concerned with one's own salvation or destiny for Nirvana and is more centered on the monastic life as a way to Nirvana. Theravada Buddhism is more interested in the early part of Buddha's life—his search for enlightenment and contentment. Mahayana Buddhism is more interested in Buddha's later life, after his experience of enlightenment and his efforts to help others along the way to enlightenment.

T HINGS TO KNOW

Bhikshu or *Bhikkhu*—A Buddhist monk, member of a *sangha*, or group of monks; also, anyone who has devoted himself to renouncing worldly pursuits and keeps the precepts and the 227 rules. The number of rules may vary. In the Tibetan tradition, it is 258.

Sutta or *sutra*—A sermon or words of the Buddha. Literally, a thread.

Tantra—Tantras are ancient writings used in meditation and rituals. They are not easily understood and have a kind of secret or magic quality about them. The tantras present *mantras,* or sacred words or sounds; certain mantras are best for certain people. The mantras are said with various movements of the body and hands—or *mudras.*

Zen—Zen is short for *zazen,* a Japanese term for a kind of meditation and concentration developed by a Japanese Buddhist leader of the thirteenth century named Dogen. Sitting upright with legs crossed, Dogen taught that one did not need words and sacred writings and rituals to achieve enlightenment. Rather, one needed only to empty his mind of thoughts, even the thought of seeking enlightenment. Enlightenment came from looking within, not outward. Dogen argued that if a person already had a Buddha-nature about him, some spark of enlightenment, one would not have to look outside and listen to others to find it. Rather, one had simply to look within.

Zen proved very popular in Japan. But actually Zen is a Chinese development in Buddhism—the Chinese *Ch'an* is Zen translated into Chinese. Military leaders in Japan liked Zen Buddhism because it brought mental calmness and peace of mind to the warriors, or *samurai*—they could empty their minds of their ego or self and then take up their mission with the sword without selfish worries.

Zen brings a sense of harmony and unity in life. Art, tea ceremonies, and beautiful gardens express the simplicity and harmony of Zen. In the 1960s, the "counter-culture" young people in the United States found Zen appealing as they sought to get in touch with themselves and draw strength from within instead of from the institutions of society. Zen makes one feel at one with nature, as well as objects at hand, whether it be a Japanese *samurai* sword or a tennis racket. There are even books in the United States on how Zen concentration can improve one's tennis game.

FESTIVALS AND HOLY DAYS

Pirit—From the Pali word, *paritta*, which means protection. The *pirit* ceremony can be held anytime, as it aims to ward off evil spirits or cure the sick or bless a new house. For seven days, passages from a special book, *Book of Parittas*, are read, usually in the presence of a relic of Buddha. This is popular in Sri Lanka.

Vaishakha Festival—*Vaishakha* is the month in which Buddha was born. On the eighth day of the second lunar month, there is a procession, which includes five levels, constructed upon vehicles, and bearing images of Buddha, bodhisattvas, and other symbols. For two nights lamps burn and music is played. The festival celebrates, in addition to Buddha's birth, his enlightenment and his *parinirvana*, his death.

Ullambana—On the fifteenth day of the seventh lunar month, particularly in Japan and China, a ceremony for souls of the departed is held. In the festival part of the celebration, temples display their rare objects. Sometimes there may also be dramas and exhibitions of objects by lay persons.

Kathina—A three-month period in the rainy season, when it is difficult to travel. Monks hold a special retreat for meditation at this time.

SYMBOLS

Buddha Rupa—There are many images, or *rupas*, of the Buddha. Usually he is seated, standing, or lying on his right side. Many of the images show the Buddha in various gestures, or *mudras*. His hands may be folded in his lap in meditation; or the right hand raised, palm forward in a blessing; or the right hand raised with at least two fingers closed; or two hands touching in a teaching gesture; or the right hand stretched down over the right knee "calling the earth to witness."

Wheel of Life—The wheel shows twelve *nidanas*, or links, that keep one in the circle of life and rebirth. There are things like ignorance, individual consciousness, grasping and "clinging," and the senses. The wheel sometimes is shown being spun by a demon, symbolizing the miseries and limits of life. In the center of the wheel are the red chicken, green snake, and black pig. They stand for lust, evildoing, and greed. Placed outside the wheel, Buddha represents release from the wheel.

THE ISLAMIC PATH

Mohamed Salomeh of Dearborn, Michigan, beneath the minaret at the Islamic Center of America Mosque in Detroit, Michigan.

"Allah is He besides Whom there is no god, the Everlasting, the Self-subsisting by Whom all subsist; slumber does not overtake Him nor sleep; whatever is in the heavens and whatever is in the earth is His; who is he that can intercede with Him but by His permission? He knows what is before them and what is behind them, and they cannot comprehend anything out of His knowledge except what He pleases, His knowledge extends over the heavens and the earth, and the preservation of them both tires Him not, and He is the Most High, the Great.

–from the *Qur'an* (II : 255)

ABRAHAM AND THE SACRED KA'BAH IN MECCA

When you think about the way people traveled in ancient times—on foot or on plodding beasts over parched, rocky terrain—Abraham was quite a traveler. He had come from way out in Ur (now in Iraq), went north to Haran (now in Turkey), then to the lands along the eastern edge of the Mediterranean. In his later years, he went south into Arabia to see a son, Ishmael, according to the Qur'an, or Koran, the sacred book of Muslims.

Muslims are followers of the religion Islam. Muslim means "one who submits" to "Allah," the Arabic name for God. Islam itself means submission to God.

Before the birth of Isaac, Abraham had fathered a son, Ishmael, by Abraham's servant, Hagar, at the command of God.

Sarah, who had no children, was jealous of Hagar and the son, Ishmael, so God told Abraham to bless the boy and send him and his mother south into the desert.

The mother and child wandered farther and farther. The great desert offered little water. One day they found they had no water. Hagar laid Ishmael in the sand and went back and forth between two high rocks looking for water. Seven times she ran or walked, desperately searching. At last she settled down on one of the rocks.

Hagar was startled to hear the voice of an angel. The angel told her not to be afraid. And at a point where Ishmael's heels touched the sand, water sprang up. This became a famous well, Zamzam (or Zem-Zem), named, some think, after the sound of water bubbling up. A town of Becca, later called Mecca, was founded there and prospered as a stopping-place for caravans.

Some years later, when Abraham trekked to Arabia to see his son, Ishmael, God told Abraham to build a holy sanctuary or room nearby, the site of the miraculous well, according to the Qur'an. They built the Ka'bah (or Kaaba), which meant "cube." It became known as the "House of God."

Boxlike, the Ka'bah is about forty feet high and about the same distance in width and length. The door is seven feet from the ground and can only be entered by a staircase rolled up to it. Inside is an empty room, except for gold and silver lamps. Much of the "House of God" is covered on the outside by a curtain or carpet.

On the southeast corner of the Ka'bah, about four feet from the ground, a seven-inch oval black stone, said to be from the heavens, has been there from the beginning of Islam. Tradition has it that the stone was brought to Abraham by an angel. They say it was once white, but the kisses of pilgrims seeking forgiveness have blackened it. Abraham, at the order of God, according to the Qur'an (XXII: 26–7), called for every devotee of Allah to make a pilgrimage, or trip, to this sacred House of God and to walk around the "house."

On pilgrimage, a Muslim starts at the southeast corner, with the black stone, and goes around the Ka'bah seven times. The pilgrim then goes to the two rocks protruding from the ground nearby. Just as Hagar rushed back and forth seeking water, the pilgrim walks and runs seven times between them.

Today the Ka'bah sits in a long open courtyard of the Great Mosque—a mosque is a place of prayer and worship for Muslims. Hundreds of thousands of people can crowd into this great open area surrounded by the ornate arches and columns of the walls of the mosque.

The Ka'bah was probably over twenty-five hundred years old at the time the great prophet of Islam, Muhammad, was born in 570 A.D. Muhammad (also Mohammed, or Mahomet in older Western usage) as a young man witnessed the rebuilding of the Ka'bah, which had deteriorated and which had been badly damaged by a flood.

About the time Muhammad came on the scene in the sixth century, Abraham's followers still honored one God at the Ka'bah, but idol worship had crept in. Some 360 idols, including idols to three imaginary daughters, called Al-Lat, Al-Iza, and Al-Muna, filled the Ka'bah. The caravans from pagan nations passing through had left their influence. The chief tribe of Mecca, the Quraysh (Koreish), had come to think that no harm could be done by being tolerant of the idols. As he grew up, Muhammad worried about the idols and decided they should not be there. Later, of course, when he became a mighty prophet and military leader, he destroyed them.

The fame of Mecca and its temple spread far and wide. Just before Muhammad was born, an invader, Abrahah, the Christian King of Yemen, approached the city, intent on destroying the sacred house and stone, which, he felt, rivaled a cathedral he had built. Raiding the land near Mecca, Abrahah seized two hundred camels that happened to belong to 'Abd al-Muttalib, Muhammad's grandfather. 'Abd al-Muttalib went to the king and sought to have his camels returned. Strangely, the king took a liking to 'Abd al-Muttalib and promised to return the camels. But Abrahah wanted to know why 'Abd al-Muttalib was more concerned with camels than saving the people of Mecca. 'Abd al-Muttalib said, "I am the Lord of the camels and the temple has a Lord who will defend it."

And defend the temple Allah did, according to one story. The tyrant, Abrahah, advanced on the back of a great elephant. But the elephant-keeper was on the side of the Meccans. He decided to give the elephant wrong commands on purpose. As Abrahah's troops began to press toward Mecca, his elephant-keeper whispered to the elephant to kneel, which it did. This caught Abrahah and his troops by surprise. The lead elephant was not supposed to stop and kneel during the attack.

Abrahah's troops backed off to give the elephant more room to get up and proceed, but the elephant turned and started following them. Not a way to win a victory! Legend has it that even the birds of the air came to drop stones on Abrahah's troops. At last, Abrahah fled. Mecca and the Ka'bah were secure in history.

NE GOD: MUHAMMAD IS HIS MESSENGER

The man who was Muhammad's father, 'Abd Allah (or Abdullah), was away during the invasion by Abrahah that ended in the elephant fiasco and defeat. But 'Abd Allah took ill in Medina, 250 miles to the north, and died. Muhammad was born several months after his father's death.

Although Muhammad belonged to the prominent Quraysh tribe, the father, a merchant, left only five camels, some goats, and an Ethiopian slave girl to Muhammad's mother, Amina. Amina, unable to nurse, put the young Muhammad with a foster mother, Halima, a member of a Bedouin, or shepherd, tribe in the mountains.

After five years, Muhammad went back to his mother. When Amina died on her way to Medina to see the grave of Muhammad's father, Muhammad was taken back to Mecca. There he lived with his distinguished old grandfather, 'Abd al-Muttalib. Muhammad was well treated by the well-to-do grandfather, but in two years the grandfather died. Now Muhammad went to live with an uncle, the oldest of his father's brothers, Abu Talib.

The uncle was a merchant also, but not so prosperous. He took Muhammad on some of his trips and taught him how to use a sword and bow and arrow. Muhammad took care of his uncle's sheep in the mountains.

When he was twenty-five, Muhammad met a well-to-do beautiful widow, Khadijah, about fifteen years his senior. She wanted a dependable young man to take charge of the caravans she sent to

Syria once a year. Muhammad got the job and did so well that the handsome young business manager and the beautiful Khadijah fell in love and married.

Muhammad continued to handle caravan business for his wife. He was active in town affairs, even sat on the council that ran the Ka'bah, as he was a member of the Quraysh tribe that took care of it.

But suddenly his life began to change. He began to feel the need to go off and meditate by himself. He left the business in good hands and spent long nights and days alone in the desert. Much of the time he was in a cave on Mount Hira, nine miles north of Mecca.

Khadijah noticed that he would go into trances, hear strange voices, and tremble. Muhammad tried to find a meaning in all of this. He began to wonder if Allah, the one God who was different from the many idols that were now in the Ka'bah, was trying to tell him something. Was Muhammad being chosen to be a prophet or messenger for the one God?

One night when he was alone in the cave, he looked out and saw an approaching figure, larger than life. As the heavenly creature came closer, Muhammad saw that he was holding a cloth with the message: "Read in the name of your Lord, Who has created all things. . . ." Muhammad was scared and ran. But before he got too far, there came a voice from above, echoing, "O Muhammad, I am Gabriel, the angel of Allah, and you—you are indeed the prophet of Allah!" Muhammad's fears were calmed and he slept peacefully.

Muhammad couldn't keep from telling others. He began to preach in Mecca that there was only one God, Allah, and that Muhammad was his messenger. The first male convert was his eleven-year old cousin, Ali, son of Abu Talib. Khadijah, his faithful wife, was his first female convert. His friend Abu Bekr, a man younger than Muhammad and also a merchant, and Zaid, a freed servant, were also among the first converts.

The going was tough. Most of Muhammad's relatives and fellow Quraysh tribesmen made fun of him. He kept up his preaching and he led prayers in houses and in caves in the hills. After three years, his followers numbered only forty.

As he went about preaching, sometimes even preaching at the Ka'bah, people began to threaten him. His uncle, Abu Talib, although not a convert, promised he would protect him, but some of Muhammad's followers who had no protector were whipped and imprisoned.

Muhammad pointed at the idols in the Ka'bah and shouted that they were just empty names. His little group began to grow.

Muhammad continued to have many visions, and as he described them, his inspired words from Allah were recorded by scribes, later to be collected and made part of the Qur'an.

In one vision, he was transported to Jerusalem, where prophets of old greeted him. In the vision he then rode a faithful horse upward into the series of heavens, reaching the presence of Allah in the seventh heaven. Here he was told that the faithful should prostrate themselves in prayer five times a day, according to tradition. The Qur'an (XVII) mentions only that he was "carried by night" to Jerusalem where he was shown "signs."

The people in Mecca, fond of their idols, now threatened Muhammad more. His protector, Abu Talib, his uncle, had died, and so had Khadijah. Although polygamy—taking more than one wife—was common, Muhammad had not taken any other wives while Khadijah was alive. The couple had six children, two boys and four girls. Both boys died in infancy. After Khadijah's death, Muhammad took a number of wives, hoping to produce a male heir—but he never did.

The prophet fled Mecca several times, but always returned. He learned of a small group from Medina that had decided Muhammad's message and his firm leadership would fit their needs.

Muhammad decided to move himself and his followers to Medina. But there was a problem in getting away from Mecca unnoticed. The leaders of Mecca didn't want Muhammad and his followers to leave for fear that they might some day come back as a stronger force. Also, some did not want to lose them because many of Muhammad's followers were workmen in the local trades and businesses.

Muhammad worked out a plan whereby he and his followers would slip out of Mecca one or two at a time over a few weeks, so they would not be missed right away. To distract those who kept an eye on him, Muhammad, with his trusted friend Abu Bekr, went south, instead of north where his pursuers would expect him to go. Hiding in caves, they at last wound their way north toward Medina. In a few weeks, his band of followers had all slipped out of Mecca and joined him at Medina. He was safe now, and his followers increased. This emigration, or flight, in 622 A.D. is called the *Hegira* (or *Hjira*, or *Hijri*). It proved the turning point in Muhammad's life. The Islamic calendar begins with this year of the *Hegira*.

Muhammad began attacking caravans bound for Mecca. This brought on several skirmishes with the forces of Mecca. In one, he was wounded in the face with a javelin.

In the year 629 A.D., the city of Mecca opened its doors to Muhammad and his growing forces. He immediately went to the Ka'bah, circled it seven times, then smashed all its idols, save one.

He left intact the largest and most revered idol, Ura. When the people gathered outside with the intention of killing the prophet for his action, he came out to the crowd and said to them: "There is no God but Allah, and I am his prophet. And the Lord has commanded me to do this. If your god is more powerful than Allah, then pray to him and ask that he reassemble those idols I have smashed." Of course Ura was made of stone and the other idols remained smashed.

Neighboring tribes began to rally to Muhammad's leadership. Soon his numbers increased and he put to field sizeable armies. In a few years they pushed as far north as Syria.

Muhammad returned to Mecca in 632 for a final pilgrimage. But on the way back to Medina, he became ill and died there, on June 8, 632 A.D., at age sixty-one.

 ECOMING A MUSLIM

There are five things a Muslim must do. These are called the Five Pillars of Islam.

First, the person must have faith in Allah. He or she shows this by reciting a short creed from his heart. Called the *shahada,* the creed is simply: "There is no god but Allah, and Muhammad is the messenger of Allah."

"Allah" is a shorter form of "Allilah," which means "the God."

There is no ceremony that brings a young person into Islam. At some point early in life he or she says the *shahada* in front of two Muslims. He or she then is considered to have submitted to Allah and is a member of the faith.

Secondly, the member of Islam practices prayer. Five times a day he is expected to stop and pray, facing the Ka'bah and Mecca—at sunset (which starts a new day), at night, at dawn, at noon, and in the afternoon. When the faithful are in the vicinity of a mosque or place of prayer, they will know when it is time to pray, especially in Muslim countries. A *muezzin* or "reciter of prayer" stands atop a minaret—a slim tower above a mosque—and announces in a piercing voice that it is the moment of prayer. Whatever a Muslim is doing, he is to stop and pray.

The word "mosque" means "prostration," a form that is a part of the posture of the Muslim at prayer. Each prayer is divided into a number of *rakahs,* or bowings. The *rakahs* each involve a series of positions, all taken as verses from the Qur'an are recited.

First, in the morning prayer (there are some variations, depending on time of day of prayer), the faithful Muslim, facing Mecca, raises his hands and touches the lobes of his ears with his thumbs. He declares: *"Allahu akbar!"*—"God is great!" Then, dropping his hands so they are just below the waist at his side, he recites the first *sura*, or chapter, of the Qur'an:

In the name of
Allah, the Beneficent, the Merciful.
All praise is due to Allah, the Lord of the Worlds.
The Beneficent, the Merciful.
Master of the Day of Judgment.
You do we serve and You do we beseech for help.
Keep us on the right path.
The path of those upon whom You have bestowed favors.
Not the path of those upon whom Your wrath is brought down, nor
 of those who go astray.*

Another chapter may be recited at this point.

Then the person bends the body and puts the palms of the two hands on the knees, and says, "Glory to the Almighty." He then stands and says, "May God accept the word of His praiser." Then he "prostrates," bowing to the floor—his forehead is in the palms of his hands as the back of his hands touch the floor—the knees and toes also are touching the floor. The person says: "Glory be to God!" He then sits back with the legs under the thighs, and with the upper part of the right foot on the bottom of the left foot, says, "Allahu Akbar." He repeats this again as he prostrates for the second time. He repeats the words of the first prostration, and then he settles back as before, saying again, "Allahu akbar!"—"God is great!"

Now, with the first round of prayers and positions or *rakahs* finished, he performs a second round, which is the same as the first, except that he may raise his hands before the prostration position and say, "O God, have Thy mercy on me." This time, after the second prostration, he sits back and declares his faith: "I testify that there is no God but the Almighty. He is alone without partner. And I testify that Muhammad is His servant and messenger. O God, promote Muhammad and the members of his house." After the declaration comes a final greeting to Muhammad: "Peace, mercy of the Almighty and His blessings be on you, O prophet. Peace be on us and on the righteous servants of God. Peace, mercy of the Almighty and His blessings be on you." While the faithful may say the prayers anywhere, saying them

Holy Qur'an, translated by M. H. Shakier (Elmhurst, NY: Tahrike Tarsile Qur'an, Inc., 1986).

Thousands of pilgrims worship at the sacred Mosque in Mecca.

49

with others is preferred. On Fridays, the faithful Muslim is expected to come to the mosque for noon prayers. In many countries, such as the United States, some mosques will hold the prayers at Sunday noon, since Friday is a full workday for many.

The head of the mosque is a layman, an *imam*, or leader, "one who walks before." There is no formal priesthood or clerical heirarchy or ranking in Islam. The imam is chosen on the basis of his dedication and learning. He will lead the prayers at the mosque and give a short sermon. Usually there are a series of education classes in which he may take part.

Mosques have a courtyard—often very long and wide. These have one or more fountains for "ablutions," or washings that are to be done before prayer. The worshipper takes off his shoes. Inside the mosque, a *mihrab*—a life-size curved niche set in the wall—marks the direction of Mecca. On the right, next to it, usually stands a plain pulpit. There is also a lectern that contains a copy of the Qur'an. Nothing is to be set on the Qur'an.

There are no pews or seats. The men line up in rows at the front, the women in the back. The walls are usually vacant except perhaps for a line or two posted from the Qur'an.

There is no music or singing, but there is a strong sense of harmony as the prayers are chanted and the prayer positions are taken in perfect unison.

The third pillar is almsgiving. Alms are things like food, money, or clothes given to the poor. As the third pillar of the faith, good Muslims are expected to give of their substance to the poor and for the work and upkeep of the mosque. Helping others is like a steppingstone to Paradise. A good Muslim is expected to heed the voice of all beggars that come before him. Even at special occasions such as a funeral or a wedding, Muslims are expected to give something for the poor.

Fasting is the fourth pillar. The fasting regulations are rigid. Muslims fast for a whole month, the month of Ramadan, the fifth month in the Muslim lunar calendar. The month marks the period in which the Qur'an was first revealed to Muhammad. Muslims during Ramadan may not drink any liquid and may not eat or smoke from sunrise to sunset for thirty days. The abstinence from water for such a long period is particularly difficult for the Muslim in a very dry and hot country. Ramadan, based on the moon instead of on the sun, as is our calendar, may come in different seasons, ranging from summer to winter.

Called the *hadj* (or *hajj*), the pilgrimage to Mecca and the Ka'bah is an experience every Muslim is expected to have in a lifetime, if he has the means. It is the fifth pillar. There are special regulations—the heads of men are to be shaved, while beards may be left on. The men wear two pieces of cotton cloth, one around the waist, one over the shoulder. Women wear five garments—a kind of trousers, over-dress, green frock, black robe, and veil. People on pilgrimage are expected to avoid arguing. They must not kill anything—not even a fish or a flea. The pilgrim walks around the Ka'bah seven times, as we have seen, each time touching or kissing the stone. Then comes the going back and forth between the two stones of Hagar.

The pilgrimage usually includes a visit to some monuments and then to the valley of Minī, where there are three pillars. The pilgrim hurls seven stones at each of the pillars. Called "stoning the Devil," the actions recall Abraham, who, when disturbed in his prayers at the site by the Devil, threw stones to drive him away. Sacrifices of animals are offered on the tenth day of pilgrimage. Those who come long distances and die along the way are considered martyrs.

Muhammad looked upon himself not so much as the starter of a new religion but rather as restoring the faith in the one God. Thus he saw himself continuing the work of the Old Testament prophets and Jesus. He recognized twenty-eight divinely inspired men of God, or prophets. Eighteen are from the Old Testament; three from the New Testament—Zacharias (in the Gospel of Luke, the father of John the Baptist), John the Baptist, and Jesus.

A lot of people do not realize it, but the Qur'an includes the virgin birth of Jesus and holds that Jesus worked miracles. Since Jesus is so highly regarded, the Qur'an believes Jesus himself was not crucified, but a phantom of him was hung on the cross, for such a death would not have been fitting for so important a representative of God.

Yet to Muslims, Jesus is a prophet—only. To them, he has no Trinity or "partnership" with God. Sometime before the resurrection of mankind, Jesus will return and rule in Jerusalem for forty years, then he will be buried next to Muhammad in the mosque at Medina.

Muhammad held that there were once 104 "God-given" books, but only four remain today: the Jewish Torah, the first five books of Moses in the Old Testament; the Psalms of David; the Gospels of Jesus in the New Testament; and most important, the Qur'an.

On his deathbed, Muhammad was asked, "O prophet, does no one enter Paradise except by the mercy of Allah?" Even his young wife, Ayesha, in whose lap the dying prophet rested his head, protested that he had a right to enter Paradise apart from the mercy of Allah. Muhammad replied simply, "No, I shall not enter except Allah cover me with His mercy!"

MEET A YOUNG MAN FULFILLING THE PILLARS OF ISLAM

Mohamed Salameh recalls that he had been outside on that special day. He doesn't remember exactly what he had been doing, but he does remember it as one of the most important days, or at least a milestone day, in his life.

On that day he accomplished the first of the five pillars that make a person a devout Muslim.

Mohamed had come into the living room at his home in Dearborn, Michigan. His parents were there, and his two brothers, Salem and Ali.

"I was thinking, for some reason, about Islam," said the tall, good-looking Fordson High freshman, who is having some luck in growing his first moustache.

Mohamed, now fourteen, was about eight at the time. Seeing the family present, he recalls, he decided to do the first of the five "pillars" of the faith: to declare publicly for the first time in the presence of witnesses the basic statement of faith required of all

Muslims. "I bear witness that there is no god but Allah, and that Muhammad is the messenger of Allah," he said.

The parents and brothers looked up, he recalls. One of his brothers declared: "Now you are on your way to becoming a real Muslim!"

Indeed he was. And Mohamed began to move on toward the other "pillars," which are supposed to be a part of a Muslim's life by age fifteen for boys, or age nine for girls. Two years later he followed the rules of fasting, another of the "pillars." He fasted during the Muslim month of Ramadan for thirty days. He abstained from food and water from sunrise to sunset.

He also observes the full regulations for prayer each day.

Mohamed achieves another "pillar" by giving alms or gifts to charity. He recently gave fifteen dollars to a Lebanese organization that helps orphans. He gives his time to others at school. "I help other Arabic kids," he says, "like maybe if they have a big test coming up, I show them ways to remember."

Actually 45 percent of the students at Fordson, which is in the shadow of Ford and other major auto companies, have Arabic backgrounds—their families come from Lebanon, Yemen, Palestine, Iraq, Syria, and Jordan. Albert Harp, one of the youth leaders and coordinators at the Islamic Center of America Mosque in West Detroit, which Mohamed attends, teaches Arabic to Fordson High students.

Mohamed, who was born in Barachit, Lebanon, wants to spend his life in service to others. Planning to be a doctor, he says, "I see the need to help people and I want to show that my life is for other people. My life is not just for me. I want to help people in Lebanon. It will give me a feeling of doing something with my life."

Concerned with fulfilling the fifth "pillar," he is looking forward, as all Muslims do, to making the required trip to Mecca sometime. "When I go," he said, "I will feel like I have done something for God."

"It's like," he said, "being born—it will purify you and you will create a strong, spiritual life."

He's interested in geography and spends his spare time drawing maps of countries.

On Sunday, he attends a special period of prayer and recitation for young people in the plain gym-size room of the mosque which is associated with the Shi'a grouping of Muslims. The adults are in study sessions. The parents have their turn in the large prayer room later, and on Sunday there is a choice of prayer in English or Arabic.

Several hundred young persons may gather at the youth prayers. As they arrive—the boys in ordinary school clothing and the girls in slightly more festive colors and wearing head scarves as required—they leave their shoes outside. They take little religiously purified clay tiles from a box. When they prostrate in prayer, they will put the tiles, called Kur'us, on the floor and touch their foreheads to the clay tiles instead of the carpeting. Muslims in prayer are not to touch anything that may have been a part of living animals.

Albert Harp, as a youth leader, directs the young people to line up in straight lines, facing him and the *mihrab*—the niche marking the direction of Mecca. The boys are in the first lines and the girls are behind them, also in long straight rows. The girls wear cloth headpieces, some of them plain, some decorative and colorful.

They go through the morning prayers. Then Mr. Harp asks for volunteers to recite from the Qur'an. One girl about ten comes forward. She recites and recites, never faltering. The hall of young people grows silent. When she finishes, there is a big smile on Mr. Harp's face and looks of surprised admiration from the other young people.

"It's a good religion," said Mohamed. "I try to show Islam to everyone. I have a positive feeling about it."

B RANCHES OF ISLAM

The *Sunnas* are the orthodox legalists who follow very closely the tradition, or *sunnah*, of law based on the teachings and practices of Muhammad. Everything is measured by the tradition. They believe the successors to Muhammad after his death were caliphs, supreme rulers or "successors" elected by Muhammad's Quraysh tribe.

The *Shi'a* Muslims believe the leadership of Muslims was passed on through the descendants of Muhammad's son-in-law, Imam Ali, the fourth caliph of Islam. Shi'a means "partisan," thus partisan of Ali. The Shi'a annual rituals still recall the massacre of Ali's son, Husain, and his followers, who fought against an army of ten thousand at Karbala, Iraq, in 680 A.D. Shi'a are more spontaneous and give considerable authority to their imams, compared to the Sunna with their rigid adherence to tradition. The Shi'a believe in free will, or free choice concerning one's fate, as compared to a Sunna emphasis on predestination, that actions are foreordained or preordered.

THINGS TO KNOW

Jihad—Muslims, according to the Qur'an, have a duty to conduct a *jihad*, or "contest" or "war," against infidels; that is, against unbelievers. Muhammad himself had suggested that Muslims not be the aggressors, and he said that the "People of the Book," Jews and Christians, should not be forcibly converted, but could live peacefully with their property under Muslim rule if they paid a special tax and followed the laws.

Muslim/Moslem—We have seen already the meaning of the word, but whether to spell it one way or another may be a question. If you live in New York or Washington, you may find it spelled "Moslem" in the newspapers. If you live in Los Angeles or Philadelphia, you may find it spelled "Muslim." Islamic scholar George Krotkoff, professor at Johns Hopkins University in Baltimore, Maryland, says there is no real difference, but since Arabic has only three vowel qualities—*a, i,* and *u*—the *u* is preferred. "It really depends on the region and the mother tongue of the Westerner," he says. "Westerners preserve the *u* as *o, a* as *e,* and *i* as *e.* Officially it should always be Muslim, but there is no difference in meaning, and Moslem is just as good."

Paradise—Belief in resurrection is very important to the Muslim. Muhammad believed that when a person dies, on the first night after his death, he has two visitors, horrible-looking angels. They question him about his beliefs: Who is your God? Who is your prophet? What is your faith? What is your book? What is your *kiblah* (the direction one turns in prayer)?

At a funeral, the imam will say, as the body is put into the grave: "O son of Adam, when the two angels come to question you, answer them, 'God, greatest in glory, is my only Lord; Muhammad, my prophet; Islam, my faith; the Qur'an, my book; and the Holy House at Mecca my *kiblah.*'"

The good souls stay near their graves. After the passage of time, the trumpet of the Day of Resurrection will be sounded. The resurrected will be lined up and tested. They will be asked how they spent their time on earth, how they spent their wealth. The deeds will be weighed by the angel Gabriel. If the scales dip down in favor of good deeds, then the person will be pardoned and saved; if evil deeds win out, he is condemned.

The Muslim idea of the afterlife is very visual. In Paradise, there are beautiful trees and gardens, fine garments, fountains and rivers, and beautiful, dark-eyed people. Most of the description is in terms of men, but Muhammad did once tell an old woman questioner she could expect to be young and beautiful again in Paradise. Hell, on the other hand, is characterized by burning winds and drinking boiling water forever.

Qur'an—The holy book of Islam, the Qur'an (recitation), is believed to have come from God himself. Tradition has it that from the beginning God wrote it and there is the original, eternal copy in heaven. It is believed the angel Gabriel dictated parts of it over a period of twenty-three years. Muhammad repeated these parts and his followers memorized them and wrote them down. After his death, it was feared that the words of Allah might be lost. A former slave, Zaid, freed by Muhammad and adopted as a son, was entrusted with the task of pulling the revealed word together. Three members of the Quraysh tribe helped. Copies of the Qur'an were sent to the main mosques in the major Muslim cities.

The Qur'an has 114 chapters, or *suras*. Most chapters begin: "In the name of the most merciful God (Allah). . . ." Except for the opening and a few other parts, the Qur'an is written in the first person, with Allah himself speaking. Muslims must be clean before touching the Qur'an. The Qur'an contains praise to Allah, stories of prophets, discussion of the last judgment, and guides to daily living and religious practice.

HOLY DAYS

'Id al-Fitr—This is a feast on the first day after the long thirty-day fast of Ramadan. It is a time of public prayers and a sermon to vast crowds outdoors. People dress up in new clothing. Presents are given.

'Id al-Adha—The "great festival," which occurs at the time of offering pilgrimage sacrifice at Mina, near Mecca. Marked by animal sacrifices, this "Feast of Sacrifice" recalls Abraham's willingness to sacrifice his son, Isaac, or Ishmael, as Muslims believe.

Aashoora—This memorial is like a somber passion play, reenacting the martyrdom of Ali's son Husain and others in Karbala in Iraq. An important day for Shi'a.

SYMBOLS

Crescent and Star—The crescent is the new moon and was associated with a reminder for a call to devotion. It was a religious and military symbol on the banners of the Turks in the thirteenth century. Several predominantly Muslim nations have the crescent on their flags; Turkey has a white crescent and a star on a field of red. During the reign of Fanouk, Egypt had a crescent and three stars in white on a field of green. Muhammad considered green a sacred color and the three stars stand for authority over Egypt, Nubia (now a part of Egypt), and the Sudan.

THE CHRISTIAN PATH

In the seventeenth century, Dutch artist Rembrandt van Rijn painted his concept of Christ teaching.

"You shall love the Lord your God with all your heart, and with all your soul, and with all your mind. This is the first and great commandment.

"And the second is like unto it. You shall love your neighbor as yourself. On these two commandments hang all the law and the prophets."

—Jesus Christ, in the Gospel of Matthew, Chapter 22

JESUS OF NAZARETH: A NEW WAY

Christians, of course, get their name from Jesus Christ. "Christ" means "anointed," or chosen of God, and "Jesus" means a "helper of Jehovah" (a name of God).

Jesus was born in Bethlehem, near Jerusalem, and lived in the rocky cliff town of Nazareth above the Sea of Galilee in what is Israel today. Our reckoning of time begins at his birth, although the actual time of his birth would be 4 B.C. (before Christ) because of later adjustments in the calendar.

Christian scriptures say that Jesus was born of a virgin woman. The miracle of his birth is what Christmas is about. The Muslim faith, although different from the Christian faith, also shares this belief in the virgin birth of Jesus.

Jesus lived with Mary and Joseph and with brothers and sisters, or rather, half brothers and sisters, as Jesus, according to the scriptures, did not have an earthly father. At age twelve, Jesus was taken to the Temple in Jerusalem by Mary and Joseph. There they lost him for a while, then they discovered him listening to the scholars in the Temple.

When he grew up, Jesus chose twelve disciples to go with him about the countryside, as he preached and taught. Among Jesus' most beloved teachings is the Sermon on the Mount, which includes the Beatitudes, or statements on being "blessed" or happy:

> Blessed are the poor in spirit: for theirs is the kingdom of heaven.
> Blessed are they that mourn: for they shall be comforted.
> Blessed are the meek: for they shall inherit the earth.
> Blessed are they which do hunger and thirst after righteousness: for they shall be filled.
> Blessed are the merciful: for they shall obtain mercy.
> Blessed are the pure in heart: for they shall see God.
> Blessed are the peacemakers: for they shall be called the children of God.
> Blessed are they which are persecuted for righteousness' sake: for theirs is the kingdom of heaven.
> Blessed are you, when men shall revile you, and persecute you, and shall say all manner of evil against you falsely, for my sake.
> Rejoice, and be exceedingly glad: for great is your reward in heaven: for so persecuted they the prophets which were before you.
> (King James Version, Matthew 5 : 3–12)

Jesus presented himself as a special kind of king, not a political one. He said he was a king of a person's heart and life. Nevertheless, his teachings stirred up jealous political and religious leaders. He was put to death by crucifixion, nailed to a cross.

His startling resurrection and later rising into heaven, as told in the New Testament of the Bible, kindled the faith of his followers. They took to the roads and to the sea and spread the Gospel, the "Good News," far and wide.

Jesus taught that his followers must be baptized, as a way to cover over or wash away sins. Christians differ on this—some hold that baptism is a symbolic gesture, others that baptism actually washes away sins for all time.

Jesus also introduced his followers to a common meal during his last supper, or the Lord's Supper. Most Christian bodies repeat a version of the Lord's Supper, with bread and wine or grape juice, but again this practice has different meanings to different Christians.

Jesus' last words before he ascended into heaven were:

"Go you therefore, and teach all nations, baptizing them in the name of the Father, and of the Son, and of the Holy Spirit: Teaching them to observe all things whatsoever I have commanded you: and, lo, I am with you always, even unto the end of the world." (Matthew 28 : 19, 20)

Christians, like Jews, share in the Hebrew scripture or Old Testament and expect a messiah, a kingly ruler sent by God. For Christians, the messiah has come in the person of Jesus.

Christians hold that the writings about Jesus and a group of writings by his followers are also a part of the Bible. To Christians, Jesus, as the son of God who came to earth, is mysteriously at one with God the Father and with the Holy Spirit—a special presence or force that continues to aid and influence Christians. Together, the Father, Son, and Holy Spirit form the Trinity. Many of the prayers and creeds, or statements of faith for Christians, reflect belief in the Trinity.

THE CREEDS

A *creed* is a simple statement or summary of what one believes. It lends itself to being repeated regularly at periods of worship and devotion.

The Apostles' Creed. This is the one most widely used by Christians. It is clear and complete and is linked, many believe, with the Apostles, namely the twelve teacher-followers of Jesus.

Tradition has it that the Apostles' Creed was written by the Apostles at the first council of the Christian church in Jerusalem.

At this council Peter and Paul argued over how much of the Jewish tradition should be carried over into Christianity.

Another story has it that the Apostles' Creed was composed ten days after the Ascension of Jesus into heaven with special help from the Holy Spirit, and with each of the Apostles writing a part.

The earliest known copy of the Apostles' Creed, as used today, is traced to around 700 A.D. However, it does parallel earlier creeds going back to the second century A.D. The "received text" in use today is:

> I believe in God, the Father Almighty, Creator of heaven and earth; and in Jesus Christ, His only Son, our Lord; Who was conceived by the Holy Spirit, born of the Virgin Mary, suffered under Pontius Pilate, was crucified, died, and was buried. He descended into hell; the third day He arose again from the dead; He ascended into Heaven, sitteth at the right hand of God, the Father Almighty; from thence He shall come to judge the living and the dead. I believe in the Holy Spirit, the holy catholic Church, the communion of saints, the forgiveness of sins, the resurrection of the body, and life everlasting. Amen.

The Nicene Creed. This was put together at the first general ecumenical council of the Christian church, a gathering of religious leaders from far and wide, held at Nicea in Asia Minor in 325 A.D. It was rounded into its current form at the Council of Constantinople in 381 A.D. The creed was an answer to Arius, a man who said there was a time when Jesus did not exist, so therefore Jesus was created by the Father. In a way, this would have undermined the idea of Christ as God. A later council, Chalcedon in 451 A.D., came to the defense of Christ's humanity as well as his divinity, saying He was one person and substance, with two natures.

In order to answer Arius, Constantine, the first Christian emperor, called the Council of Nicea, near Constantinople. The three hundred bishops who gathered listened, then replied to Arius in these words, asserting the divinity of Christ:

> I believe in one God, the Father Almighty, Maker of heaven and earth, and of all things visible and invisible. And in one Lord Jesus Christ, the only-begotten Son of God. Born of the Father before all ages, God of God, light of light, true God of true God. Begotten, not made; being of one substance with the Father, by whom all things were made. Who for us men, and for our salvation, came down from heaven. And was incarnate by the Holy Ghost of the Virgin Mary; and was made man. He was crucified also for us, suffered under Pontius Pilate, and was buried. And the third day He arose again according to the Scriptures, and ascended into heaven. He sitteth at the right hand of the Father. And He shall come again with glory to

judge both the living and the dead; of whose kingdom there shall be no end.

There are slight differences in wording (for example: Holy Spirit, instead of Holy Ghost), but basically the version is like that approved in 325 A.D. The final version of the Nicene Creed, worked out in Constantinople in 381 A.D., had this section added, and together with the above, this is essentially the version used today:

> And I believe in the Holy Ghost, the Lord and giver of life, who proceedeth from the Father and the Son. Who together with the Father and the Son is adored and glorified. Who spake by the Prophets. And in one holy, catholic, and apostolic church. I confess one Baptism for the remission of sins. And I look for the resurrection of the dead and the life of the world to come. Amen.

Actually, the controversial words "and the Son" were added some two hundred years later at the Council of Toledo. The addition has never been accepted by the Eastern Orthodox Church and remains one of the points of differences between the faiths, the Eastern Orthodox preferring a less defined relationship between the persons of the Trinity.

THINGS TO KNOW

Many words will be explained as we discuss the different Christian groups, but here are a few basic definitions.

Apostle—Any one "sent out." Jesus sent his twelve disciples out to preach; Paul, the great New Testament missionary, is also considered an Apostle.

Baptism—A ritual commanded by Jesus for all who follow him. This is a water rite that is done through dripping or pouring water onto a person or immersing them—totally covering the person. Churches disagree as to whether baptism is necessary in order to be saved for heaven. But most Christians agree on its importance as an essential act of faith or as a symbol. The word comes from the Greek *baptizein*, which means "to plunge or immerse."

Bishop—A top-ranking church person who usually heads a diocese or similar area or division of the church. The word comes from the Greek *episkopos*, one who "looks over," an "overseer."

Catholic/catholic—Capitalized, it is a part of a church name, the Roman Catholic Church. Meaning "completely whole" or universal, a lot of the churches regard themselves as also "catholic" or universal in spirit.

Clergy—Anybody who is ordained or set aside for religious work according to the regulations of a religious body; a minister, priest.

Communion—The distribution of the consecrated bread and wine at a Christian service or Roman Catholic Mass; also, "communion" can be used as a word for a church grouping or denomination.

Congregation—The collection or gathering of the faithful in a church; the church members; term also is used for religious organizations of monks or nuns; also as part of the title of Vatican agencies or commissions.

Denomination—A church body of people; usually Protestant groupings are called denominations.

Eucharist—The Lord's Supper; also the consecrated bread and wine used in the repetition or remembrance of the Lord's Supper.

Evangelical—literally, "of the good news." Churches, particularly Protestant, that emphasize preaching from the Gospels and seek to bring the "good news" of Christ to others, are described as evangelical.

Fundamentalist—One who believes in the literal interpretation of the Scriptures as they appear—for instance, the story of Creation as it is told in the Book of Genesis; although informal in worship, fundamentalists tend to be authoritarian in outlook and unappreciative of other groups.

Laity—The ordinary people who are not ordained as clergy; from the Greek word *laos*, meaning "people."

Lord's Supper—The last supper of Jesus, in an upper room with his disciples before he was crucified. He broke bread, passed a chalice of wine, and told his disciples to take and eat and drink, that it was his body to be broken and his blood shed for them. He said to continue to do it in remembrance of Him. Some church groups emphasize that the bread and wine become the body and blood of Christ in the ritual; some emphasize that there is a real presence of Christ in the elements; others recognize a spiritual presence; and some feel that the ritual today is a remembrance only of Jesus' act.

Pastor/priest—A pastor is the shepherd of a flock, so all who lead a group of people in a church or district or diocese, even the Pope in Rome, are pastors. A priest performs sacred functions, especially offering the bread and wine for consecration as the body and blood of Christ.

Sacrament—A rite or action meant to bring a measure of grace or spiritual benefit. Sacraments—some of which in some churches are considered necessary for salvation—vary according to the churches. Some have seven, some two, some none. The most basic sacraments are Baptism and the Lord's Supper, or Eucharist.

Theology—Literally, a "study of God"; the study of religious ideas, usually in terms of God's relationship to mankind.

Trinity—God the Father, Christ the Son of God, and the Holy Spirit, whom Jesus said would come and bless men and lead the faithful in difficulties, make up the Trinity. Most Christian theology holds the three to be one and equal, although the Father has a special role as Creator and was first made known to mankind.

SYMBOLS

Anchor—Another early Christian symbol, perhaps adopted because of its similarity to a cross.

Crosses—There are a half-dozen different kinds of crosses: Roman, Jerusalem, Maltese, Russian, Celtic, etc.

Fish—The symbol of a fish in early Christian art stood for "Jesus Christ Son of God Savior." The first letters in these words in Greek spell "Icthus," "a fish."

IHS—First three letters of "Jesus" in Greek IHSOUS—(the "i" becomes "J" and "H" is an "e"); also "In Hoc Signo Vinces" ("With This Sign Conquer"), words in a vision of a cross in the sky reported by Roman General Constantine before launching a successful assault on Rome in 312 A.D. (see page 84)

XP—"X" is "Ch," and "P" is "R" in Greek; thus these letters form the equivalent of "Chr" for Christ.

ROMAN CATHOLICS

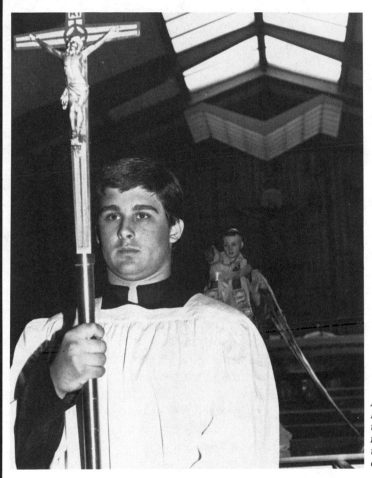

Altar boy Sam Mosca of Youngstown, Ohio, carries the cross for the celebration of Mass.

"O Lord, our Christ, may we have your mind and your spirit; make us instruments of your peace; where there is hatred, let us sow love; where there is injury, pardon; where there is discord, union; where there is doubt, faith; where there is despair, hope; where there is darkness, light; and where there is sadness, joy. O Divine Master, grant that we may not so much seek to be consoled as to console; to be understood, as to understand; to be loved, as to love; for it is in giving that we receive, it is in pardoning that we are pardoned, and it is in dying that we are born to eternal life. Amen."

—St. Francis of Assisi

OPE JOHN PAUL II: KEEPER OF THE KEYS

Roman Catholics regard the pope as the supreme leader of the Catholic church on earth. He is the successor to St. Peter, disciple of Jesus, whom Roman Catholics consider to be the first pope— the vicar, or representative, of Christ on earth. "Pope" comes from a word meaning "father." The pope is the bishop of Rome, where Peter was crucified and died.

Jesus told Peter: "You are Peter, and upon this rock I will build my church. . . . I will give you the keys of the kingdom of heaven" (Matthew 16 : 16–19). Roman Catholics take this to mean that Peter, whose name means "rock," and those chosen to take his place over the years, have been selected to lead the church and guide its teachings.

The 265 popes have come from all over the world. Mostly, the popes have been Italians; the current pope, Pope John Paul II, is from Poland.

On matters of faith, the pope can speak infallibly—that is, he cannot be wrong. When he speaks as such, as popes have rarely done, it is said that he is speaking "ex cathedra," from the chair of St. Peter.

The pope lives in a small "city-state," Vatican City, that covers an area about one-sixth of a square mile. It is a walled area of gardens and buildings connected with St. Peter's, the marvelous high-ceiling basilica, or "kingly house," the center of power and administration, where the official ceremonies of the church are held. Beneath the central altar of the basilica are the bones of St. Peter and many of the other popes.

The pope's apartment looks out from an upper story onto a square that leads into the towering doors of the basilica and the adjoining papal apartments. There are some one thousand rooms in the buildings. On Sundays and on special occasions, the pope often appears at his window or on the grounds to bless and speak to the people in the square.

Pope John Paul II became pope in 1978. A native of Poland and former leader of the church there, he is a strong, very smart man and has proven to be very popular as pontiff (meaning "bridge"— between Christ and his people). Certainly, as John Paul II journeys regularly among the continents to see his "flock," he is the most traveled of popes.

John Paul II (his name as pope comes from the Apostles John and Paul) has a background different from most recent popes, in addition to the fact that he is the first non-Italian pope since Adrian VI, a Dutchman in the early 1500s. As Karol Wojtyla (pronounced Voy-teé-wa) before he became Pope, he had been a budding college actor, worked long days at hard labor in a stone quarry during the Nazi occupation of Poland, and had been quite an outdoor man. He's fond of hiking, mountain climbing, cycling, skiing, and canoeing.

Pope John Paul II gives the traditional "Urbi et Orbi," (City and World) blessing on Christmas at St. Peter's Basilica, in the Vatican, Rome.

When the Communists took over Poland, they banned all non-Communist youth groups. Karol Wojtyla got around the restriction by taking youths on long camping trips. He made a cross out of canoe paddles and held spiritual retreats in the woods.

When Wojtyla was first named a bishop in 1958, it took a long time to get the word to him. He was off canoeing. Learning of the new honor and responsibility, he rushed to Warsaw, the Polish capital, to accept, then returned to his canoeing trip.

Popes usually remain pope for life, although it is possible to resign, as Celestine V did in 1294.

Popes are generally respected by other national rulers. Without a fighting army or world power, they offer an important voice of peace and restraint in a world of nuclear power. Pope John Paul is often heard, not only calling for obedience to traditional church beliefs and values, but also for peace and justice and help for the poor. Many of his travels have taken him to the struggling nations of the Third World.

Most of the recent American presidents have met with the pope. Ronald Reagan has met with him three times.

In 1987, at the Vatican, on his way to a world meeting, President Ronald Reagan and Pope John Paul II discussed peace. The president said he was working for "a world of justice and hope, where each of God's creatures has the means and opportunity to develop to his or her full potential." The pope, repeating a plea he had made to the president five years earlier, urged Reagan to work for peace "through greater trust between peoples and nations—a trust that is manifested and proved through constructive negotiations aimed at ending the arms race, and at liberating immense resources that can be used to alleviate misery and feed millions of hungry human beings." The pope added: "Whenever moral and spiritual values are rejected, or even given mere lip service and not truly integrated into daily life, then we, as individuals or groups, as communities or nations, fall short of what we were intended to be as men and women created in the image of God."

ST. FRANCIS OF ASSISI: POPULAR SAINT OF THE POOR

Saints are the faithful who die and go to heaven. All in heaven are considered to be saints by Roman Catholics. But the church also singles out special saints and puts them in a place of honor. These saints can also "intercede," that is, ask for help on behalf of a person, before Christ in heaven.

One of the best known of Catholic saints, and one who is loved by many non-Catholics as well, is St. Francis of Assisi, which is in central Italy, north of Rome. St. Francis (1182–1226) is remembered for his humility, his concern for the poor, his love for even little animals, and he inspired a great monastic movement named after him—the Franciscans.

But he didn't start out saintly. A lover of wild parties, the son of a rich merchant, Francis Bernardone lived at a time when people's hearts were filled with stories of adventure and knighthood. The armies of the Crusades wound across mountains and crossed seas to try to free the Holy Land from its conquerors. The boy Francis, too, wanted to be a famous knight and go on Crusades.

He had his chance when war developed between Assisi and a neighboring town, Perugia. Like a stalwart knight, he rode in a thunder of hoofs across a winter landscape to battle. He saw many of his soldier comrades die in battle. The future saint himself was taken prisoner. Francis found himself in a cramped, cold, damp prison with little food for a year. But he kept a sense of joy and his beautiful voice and his humor charmed all around him.

When Francis got out of jail, he was a physical wreck and very ill. He lay in bed for months. Gradually, his outlook on life underwent a change. He lost his zest for revelry and the wild life. But as he regained his strength, he more than ever wanted to be a renowned knight. Putting on costly armor, he set off to fight along with papal and Italian freedom forces against the Germans. On his way, however, he was disturbed by the sight of a once-important knight in rags. Francis felt sorry for him. He thought for a moment. Then he gave the knight his outer armor.

Now dressed simply, Francis stopped for the night. He had a strange dream. In it, he was promised that he would become a great prince. The next morning, as he rode off to join the forces in battle, he became ill. In another dream, he heard a voice say, "Francis, whom is it better to serve, the Lord or the servant?" He returned home, thinking about his dream.

He rejoined his riotous friends, but something was different. One night when he was supposed to be at a feast, he went off by himself. His friends could not find him at first. At last, they discovered him deep in a kind of trance.

His friends asked him if he had found a beautiful woman to marry. He thought for a moment and said, "I am thinking of taking a wife more noble and beautiful and richer than any you have seen." What he meant, he explained later, was that he had found "Lady Poverty"; he would serve the poor.

One day as he was riding, he saw a horribly disfigured leper. Most people are afraid to touch a leper for fear of catching the disease. But Francis suddenly had an urge to embrace the man and

St. Francis of Assisi in a painting by Lodovico Cardi da Cigoli.

got down off of his horse and put his arms around the leper. That experience so filled Francis with joy, that he knew he would serve beggars and the sick and the outcast for the rest of his life.

Later, as he knelt and prayed in a dilapidated old church in the countryside of San Damiano, he heard a voice that seemed to come down from the crucifix: "Go, Francis, and repair my house which, as you see, is falling down." Francis took this literally and set out to raise money to fix up the old church. Some of his former friends made fun of him, but he was persistent and got the job done. Later he was to interpret the voice as challenging him to help repair the neglected state of the whole church.

He gave everything to the poor. He even sold some of the rich goods of his father, Pietro Bernardone. The father, incensed at the turn of events, went to court to have his son officially disinherited. The court supported the father. Francis agreed to give *everything* back to his father. He even took off his clothes and dropped them at his father's feet. "I used to call Pietro Bernardone my father," Francis said. "Now I will call our Father who is in heaven my true father, not Pietro Bernardone."

Francis went off by himself, but soon attracted many followers. As he went about, he was noted for his joy and happiness. He served the poorest in society. He continued his love for animals. His preaching to the birds and animals is the subject of a number of paintings. He looked on all creatures as his brothers and sisters. He even loved things in nature. To him, it was "brother sun and sister moon," as he sang his praises to God.

Francis kept his sense of adventure. He decided to leave the running of the expanding group of Franciscans to others, and set out for the Holy Land. A shipwreck spoiled his plans, and he returned. But the disaster did not dampen his traveling spirit.

He went to Spain, then to Egypt, where the Crusaders were doing battle. He was taken prisoner, but when he was called before the Sultan, Francis preached to him. The Sultan decided to let him go. Francis continued on to the Holy Land.

Some four years later, in 1224, two years before his death, he climbed a mountain to fast and pray. After forty days—the amount of time Jesus himself had fasted and prayed on a mountain seeking to overcome temptation—Francis had a vision of a cross with a seraph, or angel, nailed to it. After the vision had faded, Francis felt keen pain in his hands and feet. He had the remarkable *stigmata*, or "marks"—the imprint of the nails on hands and feet like the crucified Jesus.

Francis was so worn out by the experience he had to be carried down the steep mountain. His health soon failed. He became nearly blind, but kept up his joyous spirit. He died in the fall of 1226. Within two years, Pope Gregory IX canonized him a saint.

Before one is declared a saint, he or she must be "beatified." To reach this stage, the life of a candidate for sainthood must be carefully investigated to make sure it was devout and exceedingly heroic. There must also be evidence of two miracles, except in the case of martyrs. The miracles are to be the result of a person praying and asking the candidate to "intercede" on his or her behalf before Christ. After a "beatification" ceremony, the candidate for sainthood may be called "blessed." He or she may be honored. If he or she is declared a saint at a later ceremony, then the new saint can be honored in the liturgy or worship rites of the universal church.

BECOMING A ROMAN CATHOLIC

The Roman Catholic Church is a sacramental church, which means there are certain signs or actions that one must do to achieve grace. Grace means the life of God in us or God dwelling in us, and with it one eventually enters heaven.

Roman Catholics have seven sacraments, or "outward signs," all of them, Catholics believe, given by Jesus and his church. Most of them apply to the ordinary Catholic; the sacrament of Holy Orders applies to priests.

Baptism. A person is baptized to be cleansed of "original sin," the spirit of disobedience with which each person is born. Original sin is inherited from the first man, Adam, who disobeyed God by eating the forbidden fruit in the Garden of Eden, and thus lived in a "fallen state." So all who came after Adam begin a life without grace.

Baptism gives one birth in the life of grace and makes him or her a member of the church, "God's family." The faith of the person asking for baptism is necessary, or in the case of infants the faith of the parents is necessary.

Baptism is performed by a priest pouring water over the forehead. As he pours, the priest says, "I baptize you in the name of the Father and of the Son and of the Holy Spirit" (Matthew 28 : 19). Baptism by sprinkling or immersion is also acceptable. There is also "baptism by blood," when a catechumen (one under instruction in the faith) gives his or her life for the faith (martyrdom) without formal baptism. And "baptism by desire"—if a person has great love for God and desires baptism, which is not available, he can be saved. The thief on the cross, having faith in Jesus but not a chance to be baptized with water, Jesus said would go to heaven. In extreme cases, in the absence of a priest or even another Catholic, even an unbaptized person with the wish to do what the church does, if he says the right words and pours the water, can baptize another person.

Confirmation. A person is usually confirmed when he or she is old enough to be considered an adult and can carry on the responsibilities of religious life. A young person usually is confirmed between the ages of twelve and eighteen. He or she can be younger or older. With confirmation, Catholics believe, comes strength, with the power of the Holy Spirit, to live the Christian life. One confirms or seals the faith present at baptism.

Holy Eucharist. This is commonly referred to as the "Blessed Sacrament." The bread and wine which are consecrated during Mass at the altar are considered to be Christ himself—body, blood, soul and divinity. Christ exists physically in the bread and wine. The Eucharist is not only a sacrament that nourishes the receiver spiritually, but it is also a sacrifice—a reenactment of the sacrifice of Jesus on the cross. The Gospels say that Jesus is a sacrificial lamb for our sins (John 1 : 29). As a sacrifice, it is like Old Testament animal sacrifices, an act of thanksgiving to God. Eucharist means "thanksgiving."

The Eucharist is the heart of the Mass, the basic ritual of Catholics. The Mass is divided into two parts. The first is called the Liturgy, or ritual, of the Word. This part includes the declaring of the words of God through Scripture recitations and a homily, or sermon, based on the readings. The second part of the Mass is the Eucharistic Liturgy. Here is the act of sacrifice in the consecration of the bread and wine and the distribution of the "body of Christ," the consecrated bread. The priest gives the faithful the consecrated wafers of bread, saying, "The body of Christ."

In Roman Catholic churches, only the priest once drank the wine or blood of Christ. But in the Byzantine (Eastern) rites of the church* which developed separately in Eastern Europe and the Near East, the faithful also consumed the wine. Today this practice of receiving both "species" is becoming more common in the Roman Rite.

First communion, the first time one takes the consecrated bread that has become the body of Christ, usually comes at about age seven, considered the age of reason, when one knows right from wrong. One is expected to be "worthy" before communion, that is,

---

*The Eastern Rite churches, largely those which were isolated in the East because of the Crusades, developed in some different ways, but later returned to the fold of Rome. Thus Chaldeans, Melkites, Marionites, etc. are a part of the Roman Catholic Church, but with some different liturgies (worship rites) and practices.

in the state of grace and in a spirit of prayer and having gone without food one hour before communion.

Penance. This sacrament brings forgiveness of sins committed after baptism. A person confesses sins to a priest, who may be out of sight in a boxlike small compartment or seated facing the penitent in a small room.

Jesus had given the Apostles power to forgive sins (John 20 : 23), Catholics believe, and Scripture also calls for sins to be confessed. Confession gives a chance for one to encounter the forgiving Christ and to be reconciled with God, the community, and himself. Very minor, or venial, sins do not have to be confessed. But they have to be watched, for little sins can lead to bigger ones.

Mortal sins, which can keep one from heaven, must be confessed. A mortal sin is "deadly"—it makes one dead to the wishes of God and dead to the grace needed for salvation. It separates man from God and puts man in opposition to God. It is also a mortal sin or sacrilege to knowingly fail to confess a mortal sin.

The person confessing may be asked to perform certain rituals, prayers, or actions to "gain an indulgence," which means taking away a part or all of the punishment that goes with the sin. Some of these actions include making the sign of the cross, praying the rosary, or making the way or stations of the cross. (See "Things to Know" at the end of this chapter.)

Matrimony. The joining in marriage, or matrimony, as a sacrament, brings the grace a couple will need to live in love and happiness. Marriage is, for Catholics, the way God expected people to give birth and have families. The sacrament lifts the state of marriage to high importance, not to be broken by divorce. Catholics quote Jesus concerning marriage: "What therefore God has joined together, let not man put asunder" (Matthew 19 : 6). The sacrament is actually administered by the two parties to each other. The priest is merely the church's witness.

Anointing the sick. Formerly called "extreme unction" and known popularly as the "last rites," this sacrament is for the very sick or dying. It brings forgiveness and increases the grace in a person's life to prepare for death and entry into eternal life.

A priest puts olive oil that has been consecrated by a bishop on the forehead. The oil is traditionally a symbol of light, strength and source of life. The priest asks God's forgiveness for the sins the person committed by each of the senses—sight, touch, taste, smell, and hearing.

Holy Orders. This sacrament passes the powers of the priesthood from Christ to the Apostles to priests today. A bishop lays hands on the candidate for priesthood. The action links one to a chain of laying on of hands that goes back to Jesus. The new priest now has the power to change bread and wine into the body and blood of Jesus and to forgive sins.

The priesthood is made up of men, as were Jesus' disciples. Priests are celibate—they do not marry. In the Eastern Rite they can marry before ordination, but a married priest cannot become a bishop. The priesthood has various ranks. A priest may be named a *monsignor* to help with special duties and administration in a diocese or archdiocese. A *bishop*, having full "complement" of orders or full priestly powers, is in charge of a diocese—the Catholics in a city and the area around it. An *archbishop* serves a larger area, usually a big city and its area. A *cardinal* is usually an archbishop named to be a part of the College of Cardinals, a sort of advisory cabinet for the pope; all the appointments are made by the pope. Many cardinals head dioceses or archdioceses. One of the cardinals' jobs is electing a new pope.

EET A CATHOLIC TEENAGER STRONG IN FAITH

You can find him at the door of St. Anthony's Roman Catholic Church in Youngstown, Ohio, greeting the faithful as they come to church.

You can find the football player at the altar, in his white surplice top and full-length black cassock, helping during Mass.

You can find him in a hospital room visiting the sick with Sister Joyce from the parish; or accompanying Sister Joyce to distribute communion to the aged who couldn't get to church.

Sam Mosca, sixteen, is not, of course, a priest or a priest in training. He is the 230-pound center on his high-school football team, Ursuline High, in Youngstown. He's an altar boy at St. Anthony's of Padua and he's in preparation to be confirmed.

All the things he is doing are part of preparing for confirmation. "We want to give a special place and thrust to the parish," explains Sister Joyce, who's in charge of religious education at this modern parish on a hill at the edge of industrial Youngstown. "We want those who are going to be confirmed to get involved in the various ministries of the parish," she said.

Preparing for confirmation over a two-year period, Sam chose, out of a list of choices, to be a greeter and to visit the sick, as he was already an altar boy. He likes helping people and wants to be a doctor of sports medicine some day.

To him, faith is another word for strength. If you have faith, he says, it not only draws you to God, but sees you through the pressure of a day.

He proved he is the strongest man on his Ursuline High School football squad. Able to bench-press or lift 345 pounds lying flat on his back, he was voted the strongest member on the team by his teammates. Playing offensive center and defensive tackle, he hopes for a college athletic scholarship some day. His own preference is the University of Michigan.

He prays with his teammates before each game, asking God to help them play to the best of their abilities. "If you have faith in God," he says, "there isn't much to worry about."

Preparing for confirmation is a long process at St. Anthony's. Over the span of two years, the *confirmands* take twelve to four-teen classes on subjects related to the faith of the church and its history and the application of faith.

As each one volunteers from a list of things to do for service, he or she must also keep a "journal" of things done to help people. Among Sam's entries are times he filled in on short notice for altar boys who couldn't get to church, and times he helped babysit little kids at church when their parents came for special classes.

He has entered the times he's gone with Sister Joyce to visit the sick at St. Elizabeth Hospital, where he usually reads a prayer from a card, and the times he visited the elderly to help with communion. He has some nice letters that the old folks have written him. One old man was impressed with both his physical strength and his spiritual strength.

In preparing for confirmation, Sam, like the other *confirmands*, has to answer one hundred questions, some of them requiring library research and an essay. There are things to memorize, too, like all the Beatitudes of Jesus from the Gospel of Matthew, Chapter 5.

The confirmands also must be interviewed one by one by the pastor, the Reverend John DeMarinis. And they attend a spiritual retreat at the church. Also, before confirmation, they take part in the sacrament of reconciliation, or confession, which most have been doing periodically since right before taking their first communion.

Confirmation is usually by a bishop, and Sam may be confirmed by the bishop of Youngstown, the Most Reverend James W. Malone, former president of the National Conference of Catholic Bishops. In the ceremony, the bishop anoints the confirmand on the forehead with oil in the form of a cross and says: "I sign you with the sign of the cross and I confirm you with the chrism (oil) of salvation, in the name of the Father and of the Son and of the Holy Spirit."

As an altar boy—Sam serves about once a month—his job is to assist the priest in Mass. Among Sam's duties is to carry a cross in a procession. Sam also holds the Mass book from which the priest reads; he carries the water and wine to the altar for mixing before it becomes the sacred blood of Christ; and at some Masses he swings a container—the thurible—of sweet-smelling incense.

Sam holds the paten, or little metal plate, under the chin of each person as the priest gives communion. Sam returns the paten and chalice and other utensils to the sacristy, or side room, after the Mass. And, like altar boys or acolytes in other churches, he lights candles at the start of Mass and puts them out at the end.

When Sam attends Mass with his mother and father—his father is a retired police detective—Sam first touches his fingers in the basin of holy water, a reminder of baptism, at the church entrance, and makes the sign of the cross. He may genuflect, that is, make the sign of the cross while kneeling on one knee, as he comes into sight of the tabernacle—an ornate container where the consecrated host is placed, usually on the altar. He may, if he enters from the side, wait until he enters the pew before genuflecting. He kneels at various times, including a moment during communion when he prays silently and examines his life, seeking forgiveness and help.

At home each night before he goes to bed, Sam asks for forgiveness of his sins, and he says, "I ask God to help me through the rough times of life."

THINGS TO KNOW

Beatific Vision—All the "blessed" in heaven will see God as if face to face and experience him in all of his glory.

The Place of Mary—Roman Catholics believe in the virgin birth of Jesus; that Mary is his mother, but Jesus had no earthly father. The angel Gabriel appeared to Mary to announce the coming of the Christ child (the Annunciation).

The Immaculate Conception refers to the birth of Mary—that although she had natural parents, she was from the moment of her conception free of any taint of original sin.

Mary, as the mother of Jesus, can reverently be called "Mother of God." She can intercede—get the attention of Jesus, so to speak—through prayers in which her name is used. In the Rosary, Catholics repeat: "Hail Mary, full of grace! The Lord is with thee; blessed art thou among women, and blessed is the fruit of thy womb, Jesus. Holy Mary, Mother of God, pray for us sinners, now and at the hour of our death. Amen."

Purgatory—Before entering heaven, souls who have died in a state of grace suffer for a while longer in order to be purged of unrepented venial sins or to make up for punishment still due in this world. Some believe the righteous who suffer a lot on earth may suffer less in purgatory.

Catholics believe all people will rise from the dead and that Christ will come on a last day to judge the living and the dead and direct them for eternity to heaven or hell for their everlasting reward or punishment.

Rosary—A string of beads used in keeping track of prayers. For Catholics, it is used in devotion to Mary and keeps count of the "Our Father" (Lord's Prayer) and ten "Hail, Mary" prayers that make up each section.

Sign of the cross—A tracing of the image of the cross by touching the fingers of the right hand to the forehead, then to the chest, then to the left shoulder and the right shoulder, saying, "In the name of the Father, and of the Son, and of the Holy Spirit." The sign is also made with the thumb on the forehead, lips, and chest. The action is a reminder of the Trinity, and the form of the cross is a reminder of salvation by Christ's death on the cross.

Stations of the cross—A devotion that seeks to relive Christ's sorrowful walk from Pilate's palace where he was sentenced to his death on a hill outside Jerusalem. These stations are shown on walls or windows in most churches—some have outdoor recollections of the fourteen places where Jesus stopped on the way to his death. A person making the way of the cross stops and meditates at each of the fourteen stations.

GREEK ORTHODOX

George Demos, holding a candle, assists at the Divine Liturgy in Holy Trinity Cathedral in New York.

"Having beheld the resurrection of Christ, let us worship the holy Lord Jesus, the only Sinless One. We venerate Your cross, O Christ, and we praise and glorify Your holy resurrection. You are our God. We know no other than You, and we call upon Your name. Come, all faithful, let us venerate the holy resurrection of Christ. For behold, through the cross joy has come to all the world. Blessing the Lord always, let us praise His resurrection. For enduring the cross for us, He destroyed death by death."

—from the Divine Liturgy of St. John Chrysostom

The date was October 28, 312 A.D., and it marks one of the great battles and turning points in history. The Roman Empire was divided among many leaders. Upon the death of Emperor Galerius, the year before, the empire was up for grabs. In Rome, the army of Maxentius, who was opposed to Christians, took charge. But a young general, Constantine, whose armies had come down from the Alps, moved on Rome. Constantine's forces were much smaller than the army of Maxentius, but he had the support of many people—especially the Christians.

Inspired by a vision of a cross in the sky and the woods, "With this sign conquer," Constantine won battle after battle, until at last he stood face to face with Maxentius at the Mulvian Bridge across the Tiber River at Saxa Rubra, north of Rome. Constantine's fast-striking, inspired troops rushed on, gained the bridge and then the city. Maxentius lost his life. Constantine gave credit to Christ for the victory.

When he became emperor of the whole Roman Empire in 324 A.D., Constantine took a direct hand in church affairs. In 325, he presided over the great meeting of churchmen in Nicea, in northwestern Turkey, the council that produced the Nicene Creed (see page 62).

Constantine had a dislike for old Rome and refused to live there. He proceeded to build his own capital at the ancient city of Byzantium, on the Bosporus Strait that separates Europe from Asia Minor. Here at the European side of the Strait that connects the Black Sea and the Sea of Marmara, he built Constantinople (today's Istanbul). The area, once under the rule of Greece and other nations, is now a part of Turkey.

Although Rome and the "New Rome" at Constantinople were united for years by the great church councils that hammered out the creeds and the doctrines of the church, the East and West saw some things differently. And as the years went by, there were some big arguments.

Among the differences was whether statues or *icons*, flat, two dimensional pictures, should be used in worship as aids in devotion. The church in the West—Rome—used statues; the Eastern Christians used the pictures, or icons. And there were the great iconoclastic, "icon breaking," controversies in the East itself; icons were banned at different times, then reinstated finally, in 843 A.D., by the Empress Theodora.

Then there were some slight differences in emphases. With the Western church the sacrifice and death of Christ were paramount. The Eastern church, while also having the sacrifice and death of Christ at the heart of its Eucharist and liturgy, held a larger sense of mystery—the altar was largely enclosed behind a screen. And the East seemed, in its rites, to put a greater emphasis on Christ's resurrection.

The Orthodox Church ("Orthodox" means "straight or true doctrine") regards itself as thoroughly Catholic, sharing the same sacraments and basically the same doctrines with Roman Catholics. One key difference is over the papacy. Eastern Orthodox do not have a pope, but an "ecumenical," or worldwide patriarch, in Constantinople, who is regarded as "a first among equals" with the Orthodox Church's other patriarchs.

The separation between East and West had been building for a long time, but didn't come to a head until 1054 A.D.

Two things in particular contributed to the final separation. There was an argument over a fine point: Did the Holy Spirit proceed from the Father only or from the Father and the Son (Jesus)? Constantinople took the first view; Rome, the second.

Then, there was the rivalry of the pope and patriarch. Two great personalities clashed—Pope Leo IX in Rome and Patriarch Michael Cerularius in Constantinople. Cerularius persisted in total independence from Rome. He closed in Constantinople the Latin-Rite churches associated with Rome. The pope excommunicated ("cut off from communion and membership") Patriarch Cerularius, and Cerularius in turn "anathematized" ("made accursed") the pope. The separation of the West and East, of the Roman Catholic Church and the Eastern Orthodox Church, was now complete.

However, in 1965, in times of growing cooperation, both Rome and Constantinople lifted the bans against each other.

Although Eastern Orthodox churches are usually distinguished by their territory—thus, Greek Orthodox Church, Russian Orthodox, etc., and these names have carried over into the U.S.—the ecumenical patriarch has often been Greek Orthodox. St. Andrew, one of the Apostles, is considered the first patriarch of Byzantium (Constantinople); there have been 269 ecumenical patriarchs there.

PATRIARCH DIMITRIOS: FIRST AMONG EQUALS

His full title is "His Holiness, Dimitrios I, Archbishop of Constantinople and Ecumenical Patriarch," and he's the spiritual leader of Eastern Orthodox Churches around the world. ("Ecumenical" comes from two Greek words meaning "all the inhabited world," thus "worldwide." "Ecumenical," more recently, has also come to mean a sharing or cooperation between churches and faiths. "Patri-

85

arch," a name used for some of the great men of the Bible, such as Abraham, means "ruling father" of a tribe or nation.)

Dimitrios grew up as Dimitrios Papadopoulos in Constantinople and received his early education at the Greek schools in Therapia. At seventeen, Dimitrios began theological studies at Halki, the Seminary of the Ecumenical Patriarch in Istanbul (Constantinople). Graduating in 1937, he was ordained a deacon and served in churches in Greece and Istanbul. In 1942, he was ordained to the full priesthood. For a while, he served as pastor of a Greek Orthodox church in Teheran, Iran, then returned to be pastor of a church in Istanbul. He became a bishop in 1964, then a metropolitan, a rank similar to archbishop, in 1972.

When the Ecumenical Patriarch Athenagoras I died that same year, the new metropolitan, Dimitrios, was elected by the Holy Synod of the church to take his place as spiritual leader of 250 million Orthodox Christians.

Left: His Holiness Dimitrios I, Archbishop of Constantinople and Ecumenical Patriarch, "first among equals."
Right: Archbishop Iakovos is the primate, or highest ranking bishop of the Greek Orthodox Church, in North and South America

Seeking to further the cause of unity, in 1975, Dimitrios set up an all-Orthodox commission "to enter in serious dialogue with the Roman Catholic churches." He sent a representative to Rome to meet with the pope. Ten years earlier, Pope Paul VI had received a visitor from the previous patriarch, Athenagoras. Anxious to heal the divisions of the years, Pope Paul VI knelt and kissed the feet of the representative from the patriarch as a gesture of cooperation.

Then Athenagoras I and Pope Paul VI themselves met and embraced in the holy city of Jerusalem—a sign that Roman Catholics and Eastern Orthodox, and indeed much of Christianity, had buried their distrust of one another.

The leader, or "primate," of the Greek Orthodox Church in North and South America is Archbishop Iakovos (pronounced "Yakovos"). Although headquartered in New York, he spends much of his time visiting Greek Orthodox churches coast to coast.

Born in 1911 on the Island of Imbros, Turkey, Iakovos grew up as Demetrios Coucouzis. He took the name of Iakovos (James) after one of Jesus' disciples. Iakovos has received thirty-six honorary doctorate degrees—many of them given him by Roman Catholic schools, such as Notre Dame and Catholic University. This tall, gracious leader has been a president of the World Council of Churches—an organization representing most of the major world Christian bodies. A strong supporter of civil rights, he joined other church leaders with the late Dr. Martin Luther King, Jr., in the historic march in Selma, Alabama, in 1965. As a special representative of Patriarch Athenagoras I in 1959 to Pope John XXIII, before Athenagoras and Pope Paul VI's meeting in Jerusalem, Iakovos was the first Greek Orthodox archbishop to visit a pope in 350 years.

 HREE GREAT ORTHODOX SAINTS

Favorite saints of the Eastern Orthodox Church include St. Nicholas, St. John Chrysostom, and St. Catherine.

Not much is known about St. Nicholas, although there are various legends which developed centuries after he lived. A quiet man, he had inherited a fortune, but gave most of it away. He was imprisoned and tortured for his faith, but when Constantine took power, Nicholas was free to live his beliefs.

He became bishop of Myra. One of the favorite stories of his kindness tells how he helped three very poor sisters who could not get married because they did not have the proper dowry, or money gifts for the new husband's family. Nicholas, it is said, dropped a bag of gold in the open window of each girl's room.

Another popular Orthodox saint is St. John Chrysostom. He is remembered as a great preacher and compiler of the liturgy, the main Orthodox worship service, still widely used. His prayers and devotional writings are also read by other Christians.

John Chrysostom was born John. The Chrysostom was added later when he became a famous preacher. "Chrysostom" means "golden-mouthed." For a number of years before he became a priest, he was a hermit, living isolated, by himself. As a priest, John Chrysostom became pastor in his home town of Antioch in ancient Syria, now southern Turkey. The priest's simple and direct way of speaking was so popular that he was appointed a bishop in Constantinople. John was outspoken, and when he denounced costly excesses, the empress Eudoxia took it as a personal criticism. He also denounced the dedication of a statue of the empress near his cathedral, so was banished to a town on the Armenia border. His letters received so much attention that his enemies decided to put him farther away in exile. But he died on the way to the farther town.

Catherine was a beautiful girl of Alexandria, Egypt. She gained attention when she went to a public forum and engaged in a debate with the leading pagan rulers. They had sought to make a fool out of the eighteen-year-old Christian girl, but her quiet and careful answers confused them, and the audience was spellbound by her words.

The persecutions in Alexandria from time to time had been fierce. Christians were hated and feared. Catherine was thrown into prison. Her enemies appealed to the emperor, Maxentius. She appeared before Maxentius and criticized him for his cruel reign and for following paganism. The emperor brought in fifty philosophers to meet with her, but they had difficulty in refuting her arguments. Catherine was imprisoned again. But she kept on converting people, including the emperor's wife, several military leaders, and two hundred soldiers. Finally, she was condemned to be torn apart on a spiked wheel, but when the wheel broke, she was beheaded. A famous monastery on Mount Sinai in eastern Egypt, the same mountain where the Bible reports that Moses received the Ten Commandments, bears her name.

BECOMING A GREEK ORTHODOX

The Orthodox have seven sacraments that are basically the same as Roman Catholics', but there may be differences in the way they are administered.

Baptism. Babies are baptized in water, but instead of having holy water poured over them, they are immersed. A priest or bishop dips the baby into a wide baptismal bowl or font. He does this three times, each time saying, "The servant of God, (baby's name), is baptized in the Name of the Father. Amen. And the Son. Amen. And the Holy Spirit. Amen." Adults are baptized by immersion as well. Some places of worship have baptistries—others achieve immersion by pouring from a font.

The baptism rite itself is in three parts: first there are a series of prayers, the reciting of the Nicene Creed, and an announcement of baptism; second a ceremony in front of the font and an anointing with the "oil of gladness"; third is the baptism itself. The new Christian receives and puts on a white garment, symbolizing a new life that will be eternal life.

In addition to baptism, the Orthodox have three other ceremonies for infants. On the first day of birth, the infant is blessed and prayers of thanksgiving are offered. On the eighth day, there is a rite in which the name of the child is given. On the fortieth day, the child is brought to the church and blessed with the mother, as Simeon blessed Mary and Jesus in the Temple (Luke 2).

Chrismation. Like confirmation in other churches, chrismation consists of anointing the forehead and other parts of the body with oil (chrism), as the words "the seal of the gift of the Holy Spirit" are said. The oil used in the anointing is a mixture of balsam, olive oil, wine, and various sweet-smelling items. The oil mixture has been blessed during Holy Week by a bishop. The newly baptized, including babies, receive chrismation or confirmation during the baptismal rite.

Eucharist. The Eastern Orthodox, like Roman Catholics, believe the consecrated bread and wine are the flesh and blood of Christ. Communion is taken for the first time after chrismation. Babies take communion at the first opportunity after baptism and chrismation. At communion, the consecrated bread and wine as the body and blood of Christ are given together to the faithful in a spoon.

The altar bread comes from a round leavened loaf, *prosphoro*, made with pure wheat flour. It is sometimes made in two layers, symbolic of the two natures, divine and human, of Christ. (Roman Catholics use unleavened bread.) On top is stamped a sacred design or seal. This part is used for consecration in the Eucharist. The rest of the bread, *antidoron*, is given to the faithful after the Eucharist and communion, including to those who did not take communion.

Penance. Confession is heard in a church or other place as the penitent and priest face each other. The priest prays with the penitent and offers counsel. Any penance suggested will not be seen as punishment, but as a means to help the person.

Priesthood, or *holy orders.* Priests may marry, but must do so before they are ordained. Bishops, however, cannot be married. Although the ordination is done by a bishop, the whole church takes part in the rite. At one point, the congregation shows its approval by shouting *"Axios!"* "He is worthy!"

Marriage. The ceremony, emphasizing the presence of the Holy Spirit, includes the placing of "crowns" on each other's heads by the bride and groom. The crowns are supposed to show a sense of joy, as the couple is united forever. But the crowns also stand for the mark of martyrdom, because marriage involves self-sacrifice on the part of each.

Anointing the sick. Like confession, Orthodox see the anointing of the sick as a sacrament of healing. It is offered anytime for the sick and not just for those facing death.

Catching the eye of most newcomers to an Orthodox church are the icons. The flat, two-dimensional paintings of Jesus, the Virgin Mary, or the Apostles and saints have a mystery about them. The subjects are solemn and thoughtful, with a background of gold or gold paint in a heavenly glow. Orthodox venerate, or honor, the icons, not for their own sake, but for the persons they represent.

A screen, the *iconostasis,* separates the altar area from the congregation. Across it are a series of large icons—usually they include—from the left—the patron saint of the church, Mary, Christ, and John the Baptist.

Three doorways in the screen give entry to the sanctuary, or holy area where the altar is located. This closing off of the altar recalls the "holy of holies" area set off for the sacred ark of the covenant in the ancient Jewish tabernacle, or tent, in the wilderness. Above the central doorway and partial doors of the screen, the Last Supper is pictured. On both sides of the Last Supper are scenes of the main feasts of the year, such as the birth of Christ, the Resurrection, and the Ascension of Christ into heaven.

MEET A HELPER OF THE ARCHBISHOP

Above his bed in his family's apartment on Fifth Avenue in a twenty-story building near Central Park in New York City, George Demos, aged ten, has a picture of himself holding open a big gold-trimmed book. A tall, distinguished, bearded man in the long ornate robes of the church is looking at the book. The archbishop of all North and South America for the Greek Orthodox Church reads as he consecrates and blesses a new bishop, Monsignor Isaiah.

It was the job of fourth-grader George to hold the book steady so the archbishop could follow. As George looked back on that day, he wondered if he had held his fingers at the bottom of the book too high so as to block some of the letters.

But the picture shows that George was doing his job just right that day in the Greek Orthodox Archdiocesan Cathedral of the Holy Trinity on the upper East Side of New York City.

There are other pictures above George's bed, and one is signed by Archbishop Iakovos: "To my spiritual son, George, with paternal blessings."

The archbishop, when he is in town, is likely to be seen celebrating, or conducting, the liturgy at the altar in the Holy Trinity Cathedral on Sunday mornings. On most Sundays, amid the candles and brilliant mosaic icons, George is helping the pastor, the Reverend Dr. Robert Stephanopoulos, with the Divine Liturgy.

The altar behind the iconostasis, the tall screen or partition, is not easily visible to the congregation, so George is not always in sight. Normally, only the priest and his aides, altar boys and other priests or bishops, go into the sanctuary or altar area.

As Father Stephanopoulos prepares for the consecrating of the bread and wine, George brings him a small, decorated, heated pitcher of water that the priest mixes with the wine, just as warm blood and water bled from the pierced side of Jesus on the cross.

At times George does accompany the priest through the central door in the iconostasis out into the front area of the church. Between the "screened" sanctuary and the congregation, there is a thronelike chair for the bishop, a lectern for the cantors or chanters to the right, and a high pulpit to the left.

At several times during the liturgy, George hands the priest his censer or thurible, an incense container that the priest waves back and forth to bless the area and the people.

During communion, George stands with a candle near Father Stephanopoulos. At the end of the liturgy George holds a large metal container full of pieces of bread from the loaf provided for consecration and communion.

George wears a plain off-white robe, brocaded with a small cross pattern. One plain white cross is on the back. Around his neck and crossing his chest he wears a stole, like a large scarf, decorated with red crosses. During days leading up to Easter, he wears a purple stole, in keeping with the somber mood of Good Friday and Holy Week.

During Holy Week, George helps out with the special services or liturgies. One is the service of blessing of holy unction, when the special oil for anointing the sick is blessed. In that ceremony, there are seven readings of Scripture. This past year George had the privilege of going to the lectern and reading a portion from the New Testament.

George had practiced before a mirror, trying to get an even tone to his reading. His father, an attorney, worked with him on getting all the words just right.

After the blessing of the oils, each person in the congregation comes up to be anointed. This is done by dipping Q-Tips into the oil. The member takes the Q-Tip home to touch any who are in need of healing and prayer.

When George was baptized as an infant, a naked baby dipped into a big round font or container, he was also anointed with oil afterward, in the rite of chrismation or confirmation. So, from infancy, he has been a full member of the church. Later, as an adult, he will assume responsibilities in the governing and teaching functions of the church.

George and his fourteen-year-old sister, Marianthi, go to the Trinity School, an Episcopalian school on New York's West Side. They are also receiving tutoring in ancient Greek.

George likes tennis and swimming at school, and according to his father he is a topnotch chess player. That is no wonder, since he practices his chess moves against a simulated game on a computer. George and his family spend their summers on Shelter Island, off the far end of Long Island.

To be a full-fledged altar boy, George went through a special rite, called tonsuring, after which he was allowed to be a reader of Scripture, except the Gospels, which the priest reads before the congregation.

Tonsure means "the act of cutting the hair," a rite often linked to initiating monks into a monastery. In a way, the rite for altar boys is a sort of a lower rank or minor order for those who serve the church, below the rank of deacons, who can perform some priestly functions.

When George was told his hair would be cut in the form of a cross, he wondered about it. "I didn't want to look like I had a Mohawk haircut," he said.

But actually only a little was snipped from the four corners of his dark head of hair, symbolizing the shape of the cross.

During a part of the tonsuring ceremony, Iakovos held the big service book over George's head, as George held the scarflike stole in his hands. After prayers over the book and George, George rose and the archbishop put the stole around his shoulders.

George recited the Lord's Prayer in Greek before the congregation. He was supposed also to recite the creed in Greek, but time ran out. Later, when Archbishop Iakovos was back for another occasion, George led the congregation in the creed.

A highlight of a tonsuring ceremony, as it is in the ceremony ordaining a priest, is the exclamation by the bishop or pastor, echoed by the congregation, that a candidate is "Axios," or "worthy." Marianthi, George's sister, kidded George before the ceremony that she would shout, "Anaxios! Unworthy!" But there was no doubt in her or the congregation's minds that day about George's worthiness.

And so Archbishop Iakovos declared that George was "Axios! Axios! Axios!" The congregation responded: "Axios! Axios! Axios!"

BRANCHES OF EASTERN ORTHODOX

The several autonomous, or independent, branches of Orthodox are united in doctrine and beliefs, but differ in some details and in the language used at the Divine Liturgy. Most use the language of their nation, although some use earlier forms of their language, as do the Greek, Arab, Russian, and Slavic (Eastern European) churches.

The branches are: the ecumenical patriarchate of Constantinople (Istanbul), Turkey; and the patriarchates of Alexandria, Egypt; Antioch, Syria; Jerusalem, Israel; Moscow, Soviet Union; Serbia (now a part of Yugoslavia); Romania and Bulgaria; plus the archdioceses of Cyprus, Greece, and Albania; and the metropolis (province, similar to archdiocese) of Poland.

A number of archdioceses of the Eastern Orthodox are under the jurisdiction of the ecumenical patriarch in Constantinople. The chief governing group for the ecumenical patriarchate is the Holy Synod. Made up of twelve metropolitans (similar to archbishops and ranked just under the patriarch) and presided over by Patriarch Dimitrios I, the Holy Synod meets once a year, hears reports, and makes decisions. The Holy Synod also elects the patriarch.

Among the "sees," or jurisdictions, under the ecumenical patriarchate is the Greek Orthodox Archdiocese of North and South America. This includes ten dioceses—eight in the U.S.; one in Toronto, Canada; and one in Buenos Aires, Argentina.

EPISCOPALIANS

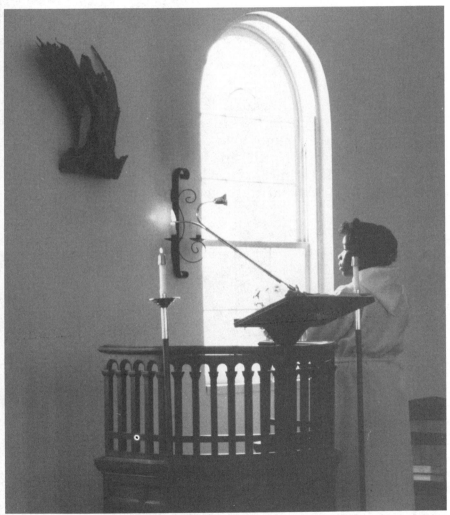

Antoinette Eason, acolyte, lighting candles at the start of a service at St. Peter Episcopal Church in Richmond, Virginia.

"There is one Body and one Spirit;
There is one hope in God's call to us;
One Lord, one Faith, one Baptism;
One God and Father of all."

—Book of Common Prayer

F inding a famous leader or pioneer more important than others in the Church of England (from which the Episcopal Church in the United States comes) is not easy. For one thing, the history of the Church of England is a part of the history of the Roman Catholic Church in England, and so, in England, the two histories go together, up to a point.

The break of the Church of England with Rome came over political as well as spiritual matters. King Henry VIII, quarreling with the pope, declared his own authority over the Church of England in 1534 in the Supremacy Act approved by Parliament. He took over church property and set the Church of England on a separate course. Yet Church of England historians argue that there was always a special kind of English church and that the mean-tempered Henry VIII merely made official what was already happening in fact.

One of the first leaders in the Church of England was St. Augustine in the fifth and sixth centuries. He was a rather undramatic man, not to be confused with the famous St. Augustine, the bishop of North Africa who was famous for his writings.

Augustine had been head of a monastery in Rome when the Pope sent him off to make Christians out of the people of England. Augustine received a good reception from Aethelbert, the king of

Archbishop of Canterbury, the Most Reverend Robert Runcie, greets the crowd outside Canterbury Cathedral after his ceremonial enthronement.

Kent in southern England. The king became a Christian and helped Augustine win other converts. Augustine built a monastery for his monks and a church at Canterbury, sixty-two miles east of London. Canterbury is now to Anglicans (those who are members of or related to the Church of England) what Rome is to Roman Catholics. It is the center or "see" of the international Anglican Communion, the group of churches with shared beliefs and common origin that includes the Church of England and nineteen other offspring, such as the Episcopal Church in the United States. "Episcopal" comes from a Greek word meaning "overseer," which was also the root of the word "bishop." An episcopal church is divided into dioceses led by bishops.

The archbishop of Canterbury is the head of world Anglicans, but he does not have authority as a pope does. He is also very important in the life of Great Britain today. The archbishop of Canterbury crowns the kings and queens and performs the rites at royal weddings and funerals. He is also a popular figure, as he visits the far-flung member churches of the Anglican Communion.

THREE WHO LIGHTED THE WAY

Three men who were burned at the stake in the decade after the death of King Henry VIII gave a force and an inspiration for the Church of England.

When Henry VIII died in 1547, his son, a weak young king, Edward VI, sat on the throne briefly. But then there came Queen Mary, daughter of a wife Henry had set aside. A staunch Roman Catholic, Mary wanted to turn things around and return England to the church of Rome. As Henry was violent, so was Mary.

In 1555, seventy-five persons who disagreed with Mary were burned at the stake. Among the victims in the autumn of that year were two Church of England bishops, Hugh Latimer and Nicholas Ridley. They were promised their freedom if they would denounce their Church of England views and pledge their loyalty to Rome, but they refused.

As the torch was put to the kindling piled around them, Latimer, over seventy years old, turned to the younger Ridley and said, "Be of good comfort, Master Ridley, and play the man. We shall this day light such a candle, by God's grace, in England, as I trust shall never be put out."

A few months later, in 1556, Thomas Cranmer, who was archbishop of Canterbury in King Henry VIII's reign, met his death. Queen Mary particularly disliked Cranmer. It had been he, under the direction of Henry, who was able to get the courts to make "null and void" the marriage of Henry to Mary's mother, Catherine of Aragon.

Cranmer had a chance to save his life by "recanting," that is, changing his mind about his faith and declaring that he was Roman Catholic instead of Protestant. He weakened and supported Mary's view for a time, on grounds that he, like many others, felt the head of state was head of the church for that country, and now the head of state, Mary, was Roman Catholic.

But when Mary's soldiers hauled him out of prison again to say once more that he supported Mary and the Roman Catholic Church, Cranmer gathered special strength. He declared he would now stand by his conscience and beliefs of his heart. He would not support Mary and Rome.

Knowing that death would be near, he promised that, at the stake, he would put forth his right hand—the hand which had signed the former recantation paper and let the right hand burn first.

And Cranmer—the first author/editor of the *Book of Common Prayer* (1549), which is the basis of the prayer books still used in Anglican churches—did just that and became a beacon of faith and courage for the church.

The differences between the Church of England and the parent church, the Roman Catholic Church, were especially keen at the time of separation. Yet today the archbishop of Canterbury and the pope meet in friendship and talk about the hope that some day their churches might be one.

The Episcopal Church in the United States used to be called the Protestant Episcopal Church in the U.S.A., but adopted the alternate name, "The Episcopal Church," about twenty years ago. The Episcopal Church remains both Protestant and Catholic.

The Episcopal Church sometimes considers itself divided between "high" and "low." The high church congregations are more like the Roman Catholic Church in practice and thinking. The low church is more informal, like some of the other Protestant denominations.

The Episcopal Church has two major sacraments, Baptism and Holy Communion, two rites believed to be especially ordained by Jesus for continued use. There are also "sacramental" rites, or minor sacraments. They are confirmation, solemnization of matrimony (marriage), unction of the sick (last rites), penance (involving confession of sin and forgiveness) and holy orders (ordaining priests).

The Episcopal Church has a meeting every three years to set rules. This convention is made up of a house of bishops and a house of delegates, elected lay persons and clergy, much like the U.S. legislative government system of a House and a Senate. Each bishop governs a diocese. Some dioceses have the same boundaries as a state, but some states have more than one diocese.

A national presiding bishop, elected by the other bishops, presides over the House of Bishops and the Executive Council, oversees the program of the church, and represents the church on boards and committees. He is the symbol of unity of all the dioceses. On the local level, the parishes each have a "vestry"—a group of members who decide on the day-by-day workings of the church.

BECOMING AN EPISCOPALIAN

A person must be baptized in "the name of the Father, and of the Son, and of the Holy Spirit," words that are said at baptism in many faiths. Baptism is performed by pouring of water or immersion. Usually infants are baptized, but if a person has not been baptized as a baby, he or she can be baptized at any point in life.

You must be baptized before you can be confirmed, confirmation meaning "a strengthening" or renewal of faith. Once confirmed, you are expected to receive communion regularly and take part in the full life of the church.

At confirmation, the candidates are "presented" to a bishop. The bishop asks: "Do you reaffirm your renunciation of evil?" and "Do you reaffirm your commitment to Jesus Christ?"

The young persons being confirmed answer: "I do, and with God's grace I will follow him as my Savior and Lord."

And they pledge to be good examples and to "strive for justice and peace among all people, and respect the dignity of every human being."

The bishop lays his hands upon each one and asks the Holy Spirit "to empower" each one for service. He asks for special strength for each to accomplish the tasks that lie ahead.

M EET AN EPISCOPALIAN ACOLYTE

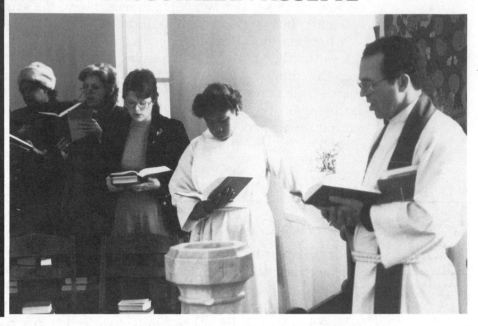

Antoinette Eason with the visiting pastor at St. Peter's Church.

Antoinette Eason, aged eleven, puts on her white robe over her red Sunday sweater and skirt and walks to the center altar of the small St. Peter's Episcopal Church in Richmond, Virginia.

As an acolyte, she makes the sign of the cross at the polished modern wooden altar, then retreats to the rear of the church, where she picks up the candle lighter. The people are seated in a semicircle on each side of the central altar.

Antoinette walks over to the lectern just to the right of the altar and touches the candles on each side of the pulpit with the long-stem candle lighter.

Light streams in from the windows in this cheerfully fresh, white-walled church. The candles flicker as she proceeds to light the candles at the altar. She returns the candle lighter and reenters with a tall, simple pole with a cross on top of it. On the church walls are the Greek letters standing for "ch" and "rho," the first two letters of the word *Christ*, "ch" and "r."

Antoinette's mother sits with friends at the back of the church. But in this church, the back is not so far away. There are only seven rows on each side of the altar. The seats are nearly all filled. And there are many young people.

The pastor (also called a rector) is away this Sunday, and a visiting priest in white robes stands at the altar. The congregation and visiting priest recite the Nicene Creed.

The *Book of Common Prayer* has prayers and Scripture readings for each Sunday and season. There are the Prayers of the People:

"Father, we pray for your holy catholic church . . . that we all may be one." Included are prayers for the leaders of the church and of the nations and for the work of the church. Time is allowed for spontaneous prayers from the congregation for the sick or for those in special need.

Antoinette sits near the altar. She stands along with the others at the reading of the Gospel, the account of the life and words of Jesus. Today the reading is from the Gospel of Matthew—5 : 1–12—the Beatitudes: ". . . Blessed are the poor in spirit, for theirs is the kingdom of heaven. . . ." A hymn based on another beatitude is sung: "Blessed are the pure in heart, for they shall see our God; the secret of the Lord is theirs, their soul is Christ's abode. . . ."

The congregation reads a confession of sins and makes the sign of the cross as the priest says the words of absolution, or pardon. Then comes the time for the offering of gifts—pledges and money, as well as the bread and wine for the communion. Ushers pass the offering plates. Antoinette drops in her church envelope, which as every Sunday includes her offering of two dollars, part of her earnings from a newspaper route.

The Eucharistic Prayer is the central part of the service as in Roman Catholic and Eastern Orthodox churches—the thanksgiving and offering of the body and blood of Christ in the bread and wine, followed by communion. The celebrant, as the presiding minister during the Eucharist is called, lifts the bread high above the altar. He does the same with the wine, recognizing it as standing for the sacrificial body and blood of Christ.

Facing the altar, he continues: "It is right and a good and joyful thing, always and everywhere to give thanks to you, Father Almighty, Creator of heaven and earth."

During the Eucharist, the celebrant repeats the words from I Corinthians 11 : 23–25: "That the Lord Jesus the same night in which he was betrayed took bread: And when he had given thanks, he brake it, and said, Take, eat, this is my body, which is broken for you. . . ."

The congregation responds with: "We remember his death, We proclaim his resurrection, We await his coming in glory. . . ."

Antoinette joins with the others in singing the Lord's Prayer: ". . . forgive us our sins . . . the kingdom, the power and the glory are yours, now and forever."

The celebrant breaks the loaf. "Alleluia," sings the congregation. He pours the wine into the communion chalice, or cup.

Antoinette stands with the others and leads the way to the altar for those who come forward, kneel, and accept the broken bread and cup. A woman from the congregation helps the priest or celebrant to distribute the bread and wine to the kneeling faithful.

In closing, the congregation sings a joyful hymn about salvation in Christ. Antoinette quietly goes back to the candles, snuffs them out, then carries the cross to the door with the priest. The service is over.

Antoinette likes being in the Episcopal Church, she says, because "we participate here in the service and everybody reads the service." Also, perhaps since the church is small, "we all know each other." She likes the church, too, because "it's not just all grown folks."

There is a time in the church service when, as in other churches, everybody stops and shakes hands. So the service is not all just listening. She says, "You can ask how your friends are doing, and other stuff."

At home she tries to read her Bible each evening. During the week she takes part in sports at the East End Middle School in Richmond. She plays center on the girls' basketball team, and she is a cadet scout and a member of the school's drill team. After school she helps wash dishes and does other things for her grandfather, who is recovering from open-heart surgery. But Sunday is a special day. "She just loves to come to church," says her mother.

LUTHERANS

Michael Dennert outside the Atonement Lutheran Church in Overland Park, Kansas.

"On this I take my stand. I can do no other. God help me. Amen."
—Martin Luther before the Diet (assembly) at Worms, Germany, 1521

MARTIN LUTHER: PAVING THE WAY FOR PROTESTANTS

At the beginning of the sixteenth century, unrest was growing in the Roman Catholic Church. People had to give a lot of money to governments and the church. Particularly, people were unhappy with "indulgences," payments to the church often painfully high, to help lessen the suffering of the dead in the afterlife. And not everybody agreed with the teaching and leadership of the pope. Those who "protested" in this period were soon called "Protestants."

Martin Luther is the man who brought all the waves of protest together. He stood up for his beliefs and dared to defy the messengers of the pope. However, Luther himself was protected by a powerful leader, Frederick the Wise, prince of Saxony in southern Germany. Unrest and revolt continued and erupted into the Protestant Reformation. Many modern Protestant denominations were formed as a result of the Reformation. But they, too, trace themselves back to Jesus as does the Roman Catholic Church.

Luther was born 1483 in Germany. As a young man, he first studied law. One day, when he was a student, he was walking along a quiet road. The sky became very dark. Suddenly there was thunder and lightning. A bolt of lightning ripped toward him, knocking him to the ground. He cried out, "St. Anne,* help me! I will become a monk!" He lived, and he did become a monk.

Entering a monastery, Luther studied and prayed hard and performed his daily duties. But he was not happy as a monk. He wanted to be perfect—to do everything that God wanted him to do. But Luther felt far from God. He worried about his own salvation. Being a monk, could he still go to hell, he wondered.

Luther worried that although he was a good monk, he still "stood before God as a sinner troubled in conscience." He said: "I did not love a just and angry God, but rather I hated and murmured against him." Then one day Luther read again the Apostle Paul's words that "a man is justified by faith without the deeds of the law." Luther studied night and day. He found that through "grace and sheer mercy God justifies us through faith," and that we don't win God's favor just by good works. "I felt myself to be reborn and to have gone through open doors into paradise," he wrote. "Justification by faith" became a banner cry of the Reformation.

In 1517, a new demand had come from Rome for more money to buy indulgences and to help build the great basilica of the church in Rome. To Luther, this was too much. It was faith that was

*Anne, or Anna, is the mother of Mary, who is the mother of Jesus.

important in trying to win salvation, he said. He stormed over to the castle church in Wittenberg and nailed ninety-five ideas, or "theses," to the door. He said things like: "Why doesn't the pope build the basilica of St. Peter out of his own money? . . . The pope would do better to sell St. Peter's and give the money to the poor folk who are being fleeced by the hawkers of indulgences."

The church attacked Luther, sending its scholars and investigators to engage him in debate. Had he not been protected by Prince Frederick the Wise, Luther might have been burned at the stake, like the Bohemian John Hus and others.

In 1521 in one great debate at the Diet of Worms, in which he was asked to recant his faith, Luther spoke his now famous words: "Here I stand. I can do no other. God help me. Amen."

Luther continued to stand his ground. Wars followed. Provinces and countries split away. New movements developed all over Europe. Those that kept to the teachings of Luther were called "Lutherans."

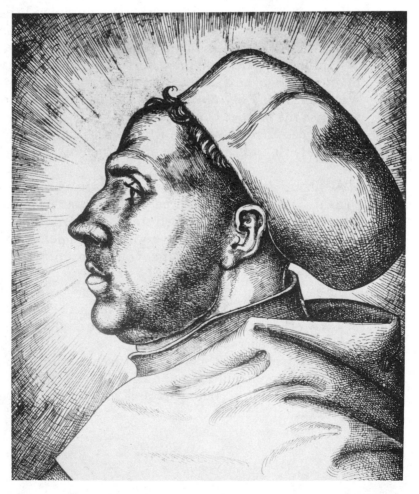

A German woodcut of Martin Luther.

BECOMING A LUTHERAN

The pastor stood in his long robes, looking out over the congregation at Atonement Lutheran Church in Overland Park, Kansas. He was receiving new members into the church, those from other churches who wished to become a part of the Lutheran congregation.

The pastor, the Reverend Charles Maas, later elected a Lutheran bishop, asked the newcomers, who had been baptized and who had taken instruction, four questions: Do they "renounce all the forces of evil?" Do they believe in God the Father? Do they believe in Jesus Christ, the Son of God, and do they believe in the Holy Spirit? They answered yes, and recited parts of the creeds.

Then the pastor said: "Let us pray for those who are affirming their baptism, and for all the baptized believers everywhere: That they may be redeemed from all evil and rescued from the way of sin and death: Lord, in your mercy. . . ." And the congregation answered: "Hear our prayer."

If your parents are in the Lutheran church and they wished for you to be also, you were baptized as an infant. The pastor sprinkled you with water or poured a little on your head.

"Through baptism we are reborn children of God and inheritors of eternal life," explained Pastor Maas to the newcomers. "By water and the Holy Spirit we are made members of the church which is the body of Christ."

He added that "as we live with Christ and with His people, we grow in faith, love, and obedience to the will of God."

At about age thirteen, a young person is expected to be confirmed. Those who plan to be confirmed at Atonement Lutheran Church receive a small brochure, a *Confirmation Handbook*, by Pastor Maas. In it he explains to the young persons who will soon become full members of the congregation what confirmation means.

He says confirmation is two things. It is "both an event of public affirmation and a lifelong process." This is to say that confirmation is a way of letting the people around you know that you're serious about being a part of the church.

As in other faiths, this rite of initiation brings the young person into new responsibilities and duties. One of these is that he or she will now be able to take part and vote on church matters in the congregation's meetings.

MEET A NEWLY CONFIRMED LUTHERAN

Michael Dennert was baptized as a baby by a Lutheran pastor. Recently he was confirmed in the faith, after a program of study and preparation at the Atonement Lutheran Church in Overland Park, Kansas.

One of the things he did in preparation, after a time of instruction, was to answer in writing a series of questions. He was asked about baptism and confirmation.

One question was: "What does confirmation or affirmation of baptism mean to you?"

He answered: "Confirmation is the affirmation of my baptism. Only this time I will understand what is happening."

He was asked other questions: "What part will the church play in your future life of faith?"

He answered: "I think the church will always be there for me. I am sure that I will always attend church regularly because I think it is important for your life to do so."

And: "How would you describe God and Jesus Christ if you were talking to someone who knew nothing of the Christian faith?"

Michael said: "If I had to describe God or Jesus to someone else, I would say that they are caring. That they are not like us, but are perfect, loving, gentle, and creative. That they do not discriminate or put down people."

And: "In what ways does your faith help you?"

Michael: "Although I am not a fanatic about it, it does have its influence on me. It makes me want to be good even though it is hard to be good at times. If things go wrong, and I get depressed, I can count on a prayer to help me."

Mike Dennert is a tall young man who likes sports and music. He played tight end for Indian Creek Junior High in Overland Park which is near Kansas City, Kansas. He is now at South Shawnee Mission High School, where he likes gym and geography.

You can't miss the fact that Mike likes music. He wears a jeans jacket covered with all kinds of band buttons. There are buttons of the Rolling Stones, Pink Floyd, Led Zeppelin, the Kinks, and others. Somehow old political buttons of Nixon and Agnew from 1968 found their way onto his jacket.

For several years Mike has been an acolyte—a young person who helps at the altar on Sundays. He wears a robe, tied with a ropelike belt or cincture. One of his tasks is to light a series of candles at the beginning of the worship. He uses one big candlestick which has an arm with a flame on it with which he touches and brings a flame to each candle. At the end of the service, he extinguishes the flames with the cuplike end of the same lighter stick.

Mike helps with the communion service by holding the plate with the holy wafers and the silver container for little glasses at communion. Lutherans have traditionally served the wine of communion in a chalice, or cup. Today many congregations have the pastor pour from a pitcherlike chalice into individual tiny glasses. The faithful take the bread, then drink the wine and return the tiny glasses to the tray.

The bread and wine in communion are received as a real presence of Jesus. The body and blood of Christ are present "in, with, and under" the bread and wine. Luther once explained the "presence" of Christ at communion is much like a heated ingot of iron—you can't see the heat, but you know it is there.

Michael, like other Lutheran boys and girls, began taking communion in the fifth grade.

Preparing for confirmation, Michael took classes over a six-week period after school in the seventh grade. These dealt with the Bible, Jesus, and modern men of faith, such as Martin Luther King. In the eighth grade, he studied Old and New Testament history and the life and thinking of Martin Luther. He also learned about the worship service and organization of the church, and he studied "ethical decision-making."

Mike took part in three weekend study camps. Then he had to choose a form of service to the church, such as working ten hours in a nursery or as an usher or an acolyte. He chose serving as an acolyte. He also helped the poor by passing out food at a church mission and cleaning food drums at another service center.

He is expected to share some of his money. He speaks lightly of giving ten dollars out of his allowance. "Ten dollars for somebody is no big deal to you, but to others it is," he said. "Jesus helped others. He gave to others, even died for others."

During the service, when Mike was confirmed with thirty others, he recited the Apostles' Creed, the ancient statement of faith that some trace back to the disciples and followers of Jesus in the first century.

Lutherans have a number of "confessions of faith" which they acknowledge in addition to the Nicene, Apostles', and Anthanasian creeds. Basically there are six "confessions," or statements of faith. Most get their names from the towns in which they were written, such as the Augsburg Confession, which was written by leaders of the Reformation in 1530 in Augsburg in Bavaria, or Germany.

Lutheran worship uses a prayer book that has service readings, prayers, and responses. The pastor sings most of his readings and the congregation also sings their responses.

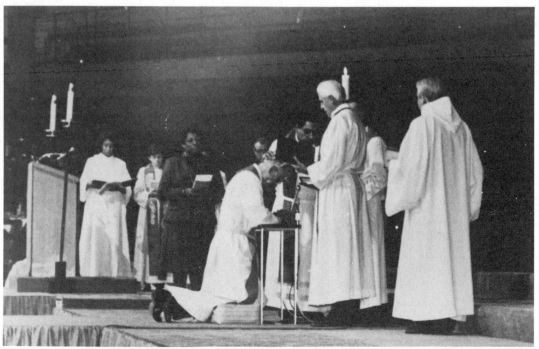

The Reverend Herbert W. Chilstrom is installed as the first bishop of the Evangelical Lutheran Church in America, a union of three American Lutheran churches, 1987.

109

BRANCHES OF LUTHERANISM

Over the years there have been many branches of Lutherans in the United States. Many of these represent the Lutheran church in the country from which they came—namely, Germany and the Scandinavian countries. But in recent years some of these churches have settled their differences and merged together.

Today there are two main Lutheran bodies. The new Evangelical Lutheran Church in America came into being January 1, 1988. This merger brings together the Lutheran Church in America, the American Lutheran Church, which Michael's congregation in Overland Park belonged to, and the Association of Evangelical Lutheran Churches.

The other big Lutheran church body with 2.6 million members, which is not joining the new merger, is the Lutheran Church—Missouri Synod. This group gets its name from German immigrants who originally settled in the state of Missouri. The Missouri Synod is conservative, holding more strictly, it argues, to the Bible, the creeds, and the Lutheran Reformation documents.

PRESBYTERIANS

Cecile Hardy at the St. Charles Avenue Presbyterian Church in New Orleans, Louisiana.

"Almighty God, we are by nature frail vessels, and our frailty is such that we of ourselves melt away, and when we become stronger we cannot stand by our own power. Grant, O God, that being supported by your power, we may indeed rejoice in the endlessness of our salvation, not indeed relying on any earthly protection, but because you have been pleased to choose us as your people. May we at the same time so pursue the course of our life, that we may not by any faithlessness exclude your grace from us, but give place to you, that we may be more and more enriched by those gifts which pertain to the hope of a future life, until we shall at length come to that full and perfect happiness in your celestial kingdom, which is laid up for us by Christ our Lord. Amen."

—John Calvin, *Commentaries on the Prophet Jeremiah and Lamentations*

JOHN CALVIN

John Calvin was eight years old in France when Martin Luther nailed his ninety-five theses, or discussion questions, to the church door in Wittenberg, Germany, in 1517.

Just as Luther shaped the thinking of the future Lutheran churches, Calvin, going a bit farther in making changes, shaped another big body of Reformation churches, the Reformed and the Presbyterian churches.

At eight years old, John Calvin was very much an adult. Everybody knew he was cut out to be a church leader and religious thinker.

John Calvin's father, a lawyer for the Roman Catholic church in Noyon, forty miles north of Paris, wanted the boy to get started right away in his studies.

An old woodcut of John Calvin.

At twelve, he was made a canon, a member of the staff of the cathedral in Noyon. At fourteen, John was sent off to the University of Paris to begin his churchly studies.

At the university, Calvin could not help hearing of Martin Luther; indeed, Luther had been notable on the reforming scene for six years.

At first Calvin went on trying to be loyal to the Church of Rome. He did not see himself as cut out to be a reformer, but as just a scholar.

At the University of Paris, he joined a very strict college, or section—Montaigu. The boys, working and studying from dawn to sunset, took vows of silence, prayed, and fasted. The severe life was to leave its mark on Calvin. We think of him today as a very bookish and not a very interesting man.

Yet Calvin was a lad others looked up to and trusted. He wanted to do his best.

Calvin's religious studies were interrupted for a while. His father, having had a falling-out with the Catholic church in Noyon, decided that his son should study law. John agreed and went home—anything would be a relief from the relentless studies and rigid discipline in Paris. Also, being a lawyer was a way of gaining wealth, so his father explained to him. John studied law for a year, at age nineteen, and mastered his subject.

But at Orleans, France, where he studied, everybody was more open. Ideas were discussed freely. Studying classical languages, John read the literature of Greece and Rome. He reenrolled at the University of Paris in theology and took whatever courses interested him. Without knowing exactly how or when, he found his mind had changed. He was on the side of the reformer.

John Calvin stayed out of trouble until a friend, Nicholas Cop, the rector, or head, of the University of Paris, gave a university sermon on All Saints Day in 1533, sixteen years to the day after Luther nailed his questions to the door. Calvin is believed to have written part if not most of the sermon. Cop strongly criticized the beliefs of the Catholic theologians in Paris. Both Cop and Calvin had to flee France for their lives. Calvin left the city disguised as a laborer.

Calvin eventually went to Geneva, a refuge for dissenters and reformers. He set out to work on his idea for a model city. However, there was a quarrel and Calvin left to pastor a congregation in Strasbourg, Germany, where he also married a young widow, Idelette.

When things settled down in Geneva, the people called for Calvin to come back. They poured into the streets to welcome him. There he developed his idea of a "theocracy"—a government where church and state are both under religious control, seen as God's rule.

There is a blot on Calvin's life: An opponent, a Spanish doctor, Miguel Servetus, was condemned to death and burned at the stake by the city with Calvin's blessing. Servetus had ridiculed baptism and the Trinity. Those times were harsh. Both Catholics and Protestants record incidents of dealing harshly—and cruelly—with those who disagreed with them.

Calvin believed strongly in the sovereignty of God—that God ruled everything.

He also believed in "predestination"—that God, from the beginning of the world, has "elected," or chosen, those who will be saved and go to heaven and those who will go to hell.

Calvin emphasized the Bible as more important than tradition and the church. He agreed with Luther that salvation comes from the free grace of God and not from doing good works.

For Calvin the church was where the word of God is sincerely preached and where two sacraments, baptism and the Lord's Supper, are duly given.

He said people can be active and religious in the world, as opposed to being set aside in monastic life. Some trace much of the American system of capitalism and earning profits to the thinking of John Calvin.

Calvin developed the "presbyterial" system in which the laity (non-clergy) and clergy run a church through presbyteries. A local church is governed by a board, or session, which is made up of a minister and elders (the word "presbyter" means "elder"). The sessions name representatives, who make up a presbytery. This group acts as a council governing a district. The presbyteries send representatives to a regional group, or synod, and to the General Assembly, the highest governing body of the Presbyterian church.

Many of the churches or denominations that came out of Calvin's work are called Reformed, particularly in Europe. "Reformed" refers to the efforts to reform or change some of the teaching and practice of the Roman Catholic Church. In the United States, the name "Presbyterian," referring to the form of church government, is common for the followers of the tradition of Calvin, although the word "Reformed" appears in the name of some Presbyterian church bodies.

Calvin continued his preaching and leadership in Geneva until he became ill in early 1564. One of his last wishes was that his grave not be marked so that people would not pay too much honor to him in death. He was buried in an ordinary cemetery, without a headstone. Today nobody knows exactly where his grave is.

ECOMING A PRESBYTERIAN

Baptism for Presbyterians is performed by pouring or sprinkling holy water, although immersion is permitted. A person growing up in the faith is baptized as an infant. Taking part in the Lord's Supper and communion comes after some instruction. In communion, regular bread or unleavened bread and small glasses of grape juice are used.

Christ is considered "present spiritually" in a mysterious way at communion, as compared to the "real presence" of the Lutheran belief or the actual presence of the Roman Catholic view. For Presbyterians, the Lord's Supper is a "visible sign" of the presence of Christ. Calvin himself compared the Lord's Supper to the sign of the dove, which was used in Scripture to represent the coming down of the Holy Spirit. So the bread and the juice are visible signs, something you see, representing the broken body and blood of Christ.

Presbyterians use the Apostles' or the Nicene creeds. Much of the thinking of the church rests on the interpretations of John Calvin's writing in his *Institutes of the Christian Religion*. Also important are the documents of the Westminster Assembly, a group of theologians brought together in England by Parliament during the 1640s when Presbyterianism was in favor in England. The Assembly wrote the Westminster Confession of Faith, the Larger and Shorter Catechism (teachings), and the Directory of Public Worship—still the guidelines for Presbyterians today.

The Presbyterian *Book of Confessions* has ten confessions. These, along with the "Form of Government," make up the Constitution of the Presbyterian church. Worship services, focusing on the Bible, are usually orderly and formal. Ministers may wear dark academic robes at the church service. Some add Geneva tabs—two sizeable white collar pieces pointing out from the neck.

A worship book or booklet is often used along with the hymnal. At St. Charles Avenue Presbyterian Church, New Orleans, a tall, vaulted building with brilliant stained-glass windows on St. Charles Avenue, a thin booklet, *The Worshipbook Service*, is referred to from time to time in the service.

The senior pastor preaches and two associate pastors, a man and a woman, bless and distribute the bread and juice for communion.

The choir in this church is in the back loft or balcony, so the sight of the singers is not distracting. The words on top of the Sunday morning bulletin say: "The service of worship begins with the music of the organ. Through its power and brilliance, may you feel the majesty and glory of God; in its quietness, His peace."

MEET A YOUNG PRESBYTERIAN LEADER

Cecile and her class with their teacher, Mayson Buffington.

She's not old enough to be an elder, a leader in her St. Charles Avenue Presbyterian Church in the uptown district of New Orleans.

But sandy-haired, bright-eyed Cecile Hardy, aged eleven, is a leader already. The kids look up to her.

They ask her to be stage director for plays and programs at Sunday school. On a Sunday before Easter, in the spring of 1987, her friends in the sixth grade at the church wrote a play on the great fortress-builder of the Old Testament, Nehemiah. They gave Cecile the pencil to write down the words—and to choose the best ones—that the class came up with. Somehow Cecile would get it right.

"She's a steady influence, always helping when needed," said her teacher, Mayson Buffington, who works during the week as a travel agent. "She sets an example for everybody."

"Cecile has always been a leader," her mother, Elizabeth Hardy, says.

Once when Cecile was very small, and the family was at church, she suddenly saw the pastor coming down the aisle in his robes. "Be quiet," she said. "Here comes God!"

Now she knows differently. "God is a spirit, somebody who created the earth," she says, and she doesn't look for him to come down the aisle in robes.

On Sunday mornings, Cecile helps her mother do projects before Sunday school with a bunch of little kids while the parents are attending the early first worship service. This day, Cecile, in her one-piece turquoise drop-waist dress with a handmade lace collar, is leading the kids in making clay symbols of crosses and plaques with verses on them.

Cecile is also a leader at the Trinity Episcopal School she attends during the week. She's into all kinds of sports. Recently she won the school's trophy for the young athlete who was the hardest worker. She has won medals for her swimming. She does it all—freestyle, backstroke, butterfly stroke, breast stroke.

She works especially hard at gymnastics. She's been rated a 9.5 on the floor mat exercise, almost a perfect score. She has placed fourth place on parallel bars in competition and also won ribbons for performing on the vault. Somehow she also finds time to play on the basketball and volleyball teams.

At school Cecile looks out for others. She hurt her neck one day, and before she went to the doctor, she made sure she gave her lunch to somebody.

Another time she and her friends discovered that the kids at another table didn't have dessert. She got her table to give some of their cakes to the other table.

Cecile has her own ideas about how to attend church, and even funerals, and her ideas are sometimes different.

She had heard an adult leader of the church one time say to come as you are and be comfortable in church. Cecile agreed and wanted to wear her cheerleading outfit to church, but her mother felt that wasn't quite what the church leader had in mind.

When Cecile went to her grandfather's funeral, she told her mother she wanted to do cartwheels, but she was discouraged. "Granddaddy would have loved it," said Cecile, her mother recalls. And her mother added, "Now I kind of wished I had let her turn cartwheels at the funeral!"

At home, Cecile takes care of two pets, a guinea pig, "Sandy," and a large Dalmatian dog, "Spot."

As if she did not have enough to do, she takes lessons at church on the guitar and likes to play "Amazing Grace." She used to be a member of a youth choir at church, but decided that with all the practice needed, she didn't have time for it.

She's a member of a private youth club that goes bowling or plays miniature golf a couple of times a month.

At school she likes math and English and enjoys using a computer and word processor. She writes for the school paper and wants to be a reporter on TV. She has already been on camera on TV, having acted in commercials for root beer and a bank.

Cecile says her prayers at night and finds time to read the Bible.

She likes the story of the plagues and how Moses escaped from Egypt with the children of Israel.

But she hasn't heard of John Calvin! She will, though, when she begins to prepare for confirmation next year. The training for confirmation is a bit different at St. Charles Avenue Church. Instead of the students all going to class together, each person who is to be confirmed meets with an elder once a week, person to person, and learns about the faith and Presbyterian history directly.

Cecile was baptized when she was six months old and took her first communion in the fourth grade after attending some classes.

Baptism, she says, "means you are a part of the church now and a Christian. A Christian is not as mean . . . and feels nice to everybody. Believing in Jesus and God makes me feel better and different."

BRANCHES OF PRESBYTERIANS

In 1958, three groups joined to form the United Presbyterian Church in the United States of America. Twenty-five years later, this new body, primarily northern, merged with the Presbyterian Church in the United States, largely southern, to become the *Presbyterian Church (U.S.A.).* This new denomination joins in cooperative projects with a number of other denominations.

A number of frontier revivals or preaching movements developed in the early 1800s. One of the more active revivals was in the Cumberland area of southeastern Kentucky. When the Kentucky (Presbyterian) Synod refused to recognize the Cumberland Presbytery's use of uneducated preachers, the Cumberland Presbytery set in motion a movement to start its own Cumberland Synod and new denomination. *The Cumberland Presbyterian Church* differs with the mainstream Presbyterians by rejecting predestination, the belief that says that a person's fate is already determined before one is born.

Organized in 1936, the *Orthodox Presbyterian Church* objected to what it called liberalism and modernism in mainstream Presbyterianism and sought to be more separate from the "world." It held firmly to the Westminster Confession and said it followed the Scriptures more literally, with emphasis on the words and not just the message of the earliest Bible manuscripts.

METHODISTS

Scott Fujita reading before the congregation of the Berkeley United Methodist Church in California.

"Gain all you can; Save all you can; Give all you can."
—John Wesley

JOHN WESLEY: SPARTAN OF THE LORD

He was five years old on that night he would always remember. John Wesley, who was to become the great pioneer of the Methodists—one of the world's largest Protestant groups, was asleep in an upstairs bedroom of the rectory in Epworth, England, near the Anglican church where his father, Samuel, was pastor.

The first hint of anything wrong came when a blazing piece of wood fell to his sister Hetty's bed in a nearby room. He heard her run screaming to her father. The boy didn't know what to think.

Suddenly the whole house erupted with flames. The father herded all the children into the garden. But he had missed one. The father tried to fight his way back into the house, but it was a raging inferno. Then they saw the boy's face in the window. Jacky, as John was called, was staring, dazed, through the glass, outlined by the flames in his room. He later wrote what he remembered:

> I remember all the circumstances as clearly as though it were but yesterday. Seeing the room was very light, I called to the maid to take me up. But no-one answering, I put my head out of the curtains and saw streaks of fire on the top of the room. I got up and ran to the door, but could get no further, all beyond it being in a blaze. I then climbed on the chest which stood near the window; one in the yard saw me, and proposed running to fetch a ladder. Another answered, "There will not be time; . . . here, I will fix myself against the wall, lift a light man and set him upon my shoulders." They did so, and he took me out of the window. Just then the whole roof fell in. . . . When they brought me into the house where my father was he cried out: "Come, neighbors, let us kneel down; let us give thanks to God! He has given me all my eight children; let the house go. I am rich enough."

It might have been just one of those dramatic events—a near tragedy, soon passed over in time. But John Wesley's remarkable mother, Susanna, saw it as something more. There must be a reason why the little boy was spared by God, she thought. God must have special work for him. And so she decided she would give him more attention, although she was very good about dividing her attention among all the children. John was her fifteenth child. Eight of the children died as infants, and two others did not make it to adulthood. Wesley's mother herself was the youngest in a family of twenty-five children!

After the fire, the family was separated as the children were farmed out to relatives and friends until a new rectory could be readied.

When all moved into the new rectory, Mrs. Wesley, often ill and burdened with constant childbearing, continued to be the teacher.

Over a period of twenty years, she spent six hours of nearly every day teaching a "class" in which no two were of the same age. When each of her children reached their fifth birthday, she dedicated a whole day to teaching the child the alphabet. On the next day she would have the child spelling the shorter words in the first chapter of Genesis from the Bible. In three months, the newcomer could join his or her brothers and sisters.

The home school reached into the evenings. Susanna once wrote her husband, who had traveled to London, about her evening schedule: "On Monday I talk with Molly, on Tuesday with Hetty, Wednesday with Nancy, Thursday with Jacky, Friday with Patty, Saturday with Charles; and with Emily and Sukey together on Sunday."

Wesley's father was a crusty tyrant of a man who could become angry with his wife Susanna over such things as her forgetting to say "amen" to his prayers. As the story goes, she refused to say "amen" to his prayer for the king. Apparently the husband and wife differed on politics. Once in debt, the senior Wesley spent time in a debtors' prison. But the archbishop, taking pity on Susanna, bailed him out.

At age ten, John left home for London to go to the Charterhouse boys' school, where he stayed seven years. He was a good student and earned scholarships at Charterhouse that would take him to Christ Church College, a part of Oxford University, at seventeen.

After five years at Oxford, he was ordained a deacon, first step to the priesthood, in the Church of England.

He started his famous diary, which he would keep most of his life. It began: "Whenever you are to do an action, consider how God did or would do the like, and do you imitate His example . . . ," and he followed with a number of rules on how to use your time.

This founder of Methodism was from the beginning very "methodical." He felt every minute should be used wisely, namely to the glory of God. He felt he should sleep solidly through the night. If he tossed and turned at night, or lay awake before getting up, he felt that was wasted time. He kept getting up earlier, until he found that 4:00 A.M. was the best time, having slept soundly through the night. He was to get up at 4:00 A.M. every day for the rest of his life, spending the first hour of the day in prayer, meditation, and study of the Scriptures.

At Oxford, when he was twenty-three, he became a lecturer in Greek and a supervisor of classes at Lincoln College in the Oxford system. When his pastor father was ailing, he went home to serve as a curate or assistant.

One of his closest companions throughout his life was his

returned to Oxford, Charles invited him to take part in a very serious religious club that Charles had organized. The other students, in fun, dubbed the club the "Holy Club." The members fasted, prayed, studied, and discussed Scripture. The student body at Oxford had other names for the club: the "Bible Moths," the "Enthusiasts," the "Godly Club," but one of their jestful names stuck—"the Methodists."

Actually the name "Methodists" was being used by the Catholics who believed that some illnesses could be cured by a special method of following a diet and exercise schedule. Now it was applied to the methodical young men following a precise, methodical schedule.

John found he could live on only twenty-eight pounds (units of money) a year by living simply, and he began his lifelong pattern of keeping his expenses down to the bare minimum and giving away the rest of his income.

John and his brother Charles went to the American colony of Georgia as missionaries, but had a difficult time getting along with the people, a mixed bag of stuffy socialites and poor immigrants, some of them escaped from the British prison system. John's heart was broken in romance—he stalled too long and the young woman married another suitor. He returned to England a discouraged man.

However, on his journey to America, John Wesley had come into contact on shipboard with the Moravians from Germany. He was later to visit their community in Germany. Their spirituality, calmness, and sincerity of faith eventually left a profound mark on the young man. He learned there was something missing in his life. He wanted to serve God, but realized he was a boring, rigid person. Missing was any fire in his soul.

Then, on Wednesday, May 24, 1738, he was invited to a small London religious society meeting in a home on Aldersgate Street. A writing of Martin Luther was to be read. Luther himself had been strangely warmed in reading St. Paul's words on the importance of faith alone, and not of works, in finding salvation. What happened to Wesley at Aldersgate is recorded in his diary:

> In the evening I went very unwillingly to a society in Aldersgate Street, where one was reading Luther's preface to the Epistle to the Romans. About a quarter before nine, while he was describing the change which God works in the heart through faith in Christ, I felt my heart strangely warmed. I felt I did trust in Christ, Christ alone, for salvation: And an assurance was given me, that He had taken away my sins, even mine, and saved me from the law of sin and of death.

Right away John wanted to share his new experience with brother Charles, who, it so happened, had a similar heart-warming experi-

John Wesley on the streets, in a painting by W. Hatherell.

ence three days earlier. Charles wrote later: "Towards ten, my brother was brought in triumph by a troop of our friends and declared, 'I believe!' We sang the hymn with great joy, and parted with prayer."

John Wesley's life continued to take a turn when he ran into George Whitefield, who had been a member of the original Oxford "Holy Club." Whitefield also had been to Georgia, and unlike the Wesleys had had great success there as a preacher. Now Whitefield was conducting great open-air rallies near factories and coal fields, drawing crowds of thousands of people. Benjamin Franklin, who once had heard Whitefield, said the preacher's voice was so strong it could be heard across the hills by thirty thousand persons.

Whitefield invited Wesley to join in preaching to the crowds. So began the growth of Methodism. Despite persecution and encounters with groups of thugs that threatened his life, Wesley in his black suit, without any color or flair in his appearance, preached up a storm in the coal fields. Church authorities were jealous of his success and were behind some of the attempts to silence him. Wesley, year after year, traveled over eight thousand miles, most of it on horseback, reading books all the time, not wasting a minute of his life.

He never really broke with the Church of England and even scheduled his meetings so they would not conflict with scheduled Anglican services. However, churches and bishops excluded him from preaching and this was one reason for preaching outdoors. When a bishop criticized him for preaching where he was not assigned to a parish, he declared: "Sir, I look upon the whole world as my parish."

Wesley developed a group of lay preachers, but left the administration of the sacraments to the Anglican clergy.

By 1789, two years before his death, there were nearly fifty-seven thousand members of Methodist societies. After his death, as the numbers grew and as Anglican clergy began to refuse to give communion to Methodists, the Methodists began receiving communion in their own chapels, and services were allowed to be held at times of the Anglican services. It was not until 1836 that the "conference," an annual meeting that Wesley organized in 1744 with cooperating Anglican clergy and lay preachers, began ordaining their own pastors.

In living the Christian life, Wesley felt some form of Christian "perfection" or "holiness" could be achieved. Some call it "sanctification," which comes from words meaning "make holy." Some groups, such as the "Holiness denominations" and some smaller Methodist congregations, emphasize the attaining of sanctification or holiness, or sense of living perfectly in the faith, as another special experience in the life of the Christian.

Wesley talked of perfect love, the kind that, as Jesus said, makes the Christian love God with all his heart and his neighbor likewise. Wesley felt this state of discipleship could be attained in the workaday world and not necessarily in a monastery or a cloistered (closed) convent.

Wesley recalled Jesus' words: "Be you therefore perfect, even as your Father which is in heaven is perfect" (Matthew 5 : 48). He felt that Christians could be perfect to the extent that they would be free from "outward" sin. They could still make mistakes and face temptation, but could control their tempers and their desires. Whoever experiences sanctification, John Wesley said, would have a clear idea of what God has done in a person's life. "It is," he said, "to have 'the mind which was in Christ,' and to 'walk as He walked'; . . . In other words, to be inwardly and outwardly devoted to God; all devoted in heart and life."

He continued preaching to within two weeks of his death at age eighty-eight in 1791. His last letter was to a young preacher, William Wilberforce, who was beginning to denounce slavery in the newly formed American nation. Wesley praised Wilberforce for his "glorious enterprise in opposing that execrable villainy which is the scandal of religion, of England, and of human nature. . . . Go on, in the name of God, and in the power of His might, until even American slavery, the vilest that ever saw the sun, shall vanish away before it." Thus was sounded a triumphant note of urgent concern for people, in keeping with his days of ministry in the neglected coal fields of England. The social ministry, as it is called, dealing with the issues of the day and needs of people, continues to be an emphasis of Methodists—particularly in the large United Methodist denomination today.

BECOMING A METHODIST

Methodists have two sacraments, as compared to seven for Roman Catholics and Eastern Orthodox.

"Sacraments ordained of Christ," says the *Discipline*, a thick book of rules and guidelines for members of the United Methodist Church, "are not only badges or tokens" of peoples' belief in Christ, "but rather they are certain signs of grace," of God working "invisibly in us." Baptism is the sign of "the new birth"; the Lord's Supper is a "sign of the love that Christians ought to have among themselves one to another" and "a sacrament of our redemption by Christ's death." The Lord's Supper is a taking part in the body and blood of Christ "in a heavenly and spiritual manner" through faith.

Baptism is performed by sprinkling water, but Methodists also accept pouring and immersion.

The church, according to the *Discipline*, holds that all children are already members of the Kingdom of God and are entitled to baptism. Salvation is by faith at the age of reason, the age when one begins to do his or her own thinking. The baptism of infants is a special occasion for the parents. A minister is to urge "all parents to dedicate their children to the Lord in Baptism as early as convenient, and before Baptism is administered, he shall diligently instruct the parents regarding the vows which they assume in this Sacrament." Parents are to bring the youngsters up "in conformity to the Word of God." The children after baptism are enrolled as "preparatory members." After "a proper course of training" through the church's Sunday school and other classes, a person can be received into full membership.

There is a confirmation rite for young people, symbolizing the completion of training and readiness for full church membership. Church leaders debate what is the best age, but traditionally this has been around the sixth grade. Confirmation, however, is not necessary for membership.

Membership in the United Methodist Church—the largest Methodist church in the United States and the second largest of all U.S. Protestant denominations (after the Southern Baptists)—includes "all baptized persons who have come into membership by confession of faith or transfer" in good standing from other churches.

Membership officially depends on answering "I do" or "I will" to five basic questions, in the presence of the congregation:

1. Do you here, in the presence of God, and of this congregation, renew the solemn promise and vow that you made, or that was made in your name, at your baptism?
2. Do you confess Jesus Christ as your Lord and Savior and pledge your allegiance to his kingdom?
3. Do you receive and profess the Christian faith as contained in the Scriptures of the Old and New Testaments?
4. Do you promise according to the grace given you to live a Christian life and always remain a faithful member of Christ's holy church?
5. Will you be loyal to the United Methodist Church, and uphold it by your prayers, your presence, your gifts, and your service?

Methodists have what has been called a "connectional" system. The local churches are not independent, but are connected to and under the authority of the bishop. However, each church has its own council on ministries to govern the church's program and outreach ministries, an administration board to handle finances and other administrative matters, and trustees to hold the church property. Pastors are appointed each year by the bishop at the annual conference, a legislative group made up of lay and clergy delegates.

The bishop serves an "area," which is composed of several annual conferences. The supreme body is the General Conference, which is made up of between six hundred and one thousand delegates, divided evenly between lay and clergy. It is this body that decides the guidelines and direction of the church every four years.

There are also jurisdictional or regional conferences, which elect bishops; a council of bishops, which meets twice a year, entrusted with certain responsibilities between the General Conferences; and a Judicial Council, a kind of supreme court of the church.

MEET A YOUNG LEADER WITH A MELLOW VOICE

Scott Fujita helps to serve, as the young people of his church entertain senior citizens.

On Sunday morning, when Scott Fujita enters the sanctuary of Berkeley United Methodist Church, Berkeley, California, he sits in the front pew directly before the pulpit. A dozen of his friends join him.

Scott walks so confidently to the front of the church that most people would not notice that he is legally blind in one eye and suffers from glaucoma in the other.

Scott is a sharp young man who chooses just the right words to get his thoughts across. At church, Scott is depended on to represent youth issues before the congregation. "He understands what's needed and speaks about it in clear ways that endear adults to him," according to his Methodist youth advisor, Derek Nagano. Around the Berkeley United Methodist Church, Scott is jokingly called "the voice of Methodist youth."

At El Cerrito High School, where he is a junior, Scott is a disk jockey on the high school radio station. He programs music ranging from heavy metal to rap and is known for his "mellow voice" as he speaks out on issues of concern to teens.

He speaks so well that sometimes he speaks too long. When he was asked to make a brief report to the congregation about the Asian-American Methodist Camp, Scott is embarrassed to recall how the church members kidded him good-naturedly for his long-windedness. His "five-minute report" went on for twenty-five enthusiastic minutes in the middle of Sunday worship.

Summer youth camps have always been a vital part of Scott Fujita's experience as a Methodist, and they contribute to his enthusiasm about the Christian faith. Since he was twelve, he has attended Northern California Methodist Junior High Camp.

The summer he was sixteen, Scott served as a counselor on the staff. The theme was "The Gift of Giving" and the staff wrote the curriculum. "Even though we deliver the theme and are supposed to be perfect, we're not," says Scott. "All of us can give, and all of us are selfish, even the counselors. We learned a lot about ourselves that summer."

Spending a week in the mountains with forty or fifty campers is great, Scott reports. "We get to meet and know others just like us. We are all together as one. It's great to be with people just like us. We don't feel so different, and being at camp together lets us feel more open. Camp brings more out of who we really are."

Asian-American Methodist Camp is fun for Scott, too, but it is much larger. More than two hundred Chinese, Korean, Thai, Vietnamese, Cambodian, and Japanese youth come from throughout California to camp in the Sierra Nevada Mountains. Ages range from eighth grade to early college, but many activities occur in small groups of twenty-five people of similar ages. Morning worship, skits, and songs are the high points of Asian-American Camp for Scott.

Baptized at Berkeley United Methodist Church as an infant, Scott has always attended Sunday school and worship. "Now I go because it is important to me," he says. "My parents don't even have to say 'Come on, let's go to church' any more. I like to learn about the Bible and God. I especially like to find ways that the commandments relate to us, ways that we can apply Jesus' teachings to our own lives. That's what we learn in our high school Sunday school class."

United Methodist Youth Fellowship is also an important part of Scott's faith experience. UMYF meets on Sunday evenings, and is more informal. "It helps us personally," he says. "Our group has some personality conflicts. People get down on each other for little things, but our discussions help us relate our problems as individuals to the Bible, and our troubles as a group to God."

During May each year, the Youth Fellowship leads a worship service for the whole congregation. Scott has some ideas about ways to make the worship more lively this year. As he contributes to planning the Youth Sunday service, his voice brightens. "We're going to involve the congregation more," he says. "During the time called 'The Church Family in Prayer,' the same people usually speak about joys, concerns, and needs. In the Youth worship, we're going to involve everybody. After some time for confession and silent prayer, we're going to invite everybody to say 'Forgive me, God,' together."

Scott Fujita brings energy, joy, and vitality to his church. There are many challenges ahead for him as "the voice of Methodist youth" in his congregation.

BRANCHES OF METHODISTS

A very strictly disciplined group, the *Free Methodist Church of North America* tries to follow Wesley's teachings as closely as possible. Members are expected to have an experience of forgiveness of sins and an experience of "sanctification" of the spirit, filling and guiding every part of their lives. Bishops are elected every four years.

A merger in 1968 brought together the Wesleyan Methodist Church and the Pilgrim Holiness Church to form the *Wesleyan Church*. Here also is an emphasis on "holiness," sanctification of the faithful, and the personal return of Jesus. A general conference sets the policies and elects an overall general superintendent.

Richard Allen, a former slave who became a successful businessman and lay preacher, led blacks into a separate denomination when whites insisted on segregating blacks into the balcony in the Methodist churches. The *African Methodist Episcopal Church* was formed in Philadelphia in November of 1787, just two months after the U.S. Constitution was approved. Organization—with bishops and General Conference—and beliefs are similar to other Methodist groups. When blacks were discriminated against by whites in New York City Methodist churches in 1796, the *African Methodist Episcopal Zion Church* was formed. In the South, after the emancipation of slaves and the end of the Civil War, blacks formed the Colored Methodist Episcopal Church, now known as the *Christian Methodist Episcopal Church.*

Members of the *Congregational Methodist Church* call their own pastors rather than receive them by appointment of bishops. Laymen have a greater role. They use only the King James Version of the Bible and believe in the return of Jesus and his one-thousand-year reign on earth.

Formed in 1965, in Jackson, Mississippi, the *Association of Independent Methodists* objected to Methodist emphasis on social action and civil rights. Guidelines of the Association call for "racial pride," separation of the races, and separation of church and state.

BAPTISTS

Julie Baldridge with her little sister, Amy, and their mother, take communion at Judson Baptist Church in Minneapolis.

"Having been led as we believe by the Spirit of God to receive the Lord Jesus Christ as our Saviour; and, on the profession of our faith, having been baptized into the name of the Father, and of the Son, and of the Holy Spirit, we do now, in the presence of God, angels, and this assembly, most solemnly and joyfully enter into covenant with one another, as one body in Christ.

We engage, therefore, by the aid of the Holy Spirit to walk together in Christian love. . . .

We also engage to maintain family and secret devotions; to religiously educate our children. . . .

We further engage to watch over one another in brotherly love; to remember each other in prayer; to aid each other in sickness and distress; to cultivate Christian sympathy in feeling and courtesy in speech; to be slow to take offense, but always ready for reconciliation, and, mindful of the rules of our Saviour, to secure it without delay. . . ."

—a commonly used Baptist Church covenant

OGER WILLIAMS: COLONIAL PIONEER OF FREEDOM

He wasn't exactly a Baptist, but he organized the first Baptist church in the colonies and the hemisphere.

He wasn't really a politician or statesman, yet he launched the city of Providence and the colony of Rhode Island.

He is Roger Williams, a friend of Indians, with whom he lived at times, and friend of leading personalities in the English government. He was an angry young man, always on the move, never really content with one religion or another, always searching—so much that he came to regard himself as only a "seeker."

He was born about 1604—nobody really knows the date of his birth, and strangely, the date of his death in March 1684 was not recorded either.

The Baptists were just beginning to organize as a movement about the time of Williams' childhood in England.

Baptists, like all Christian groups, have roots in churches and groups going back to the time of Christ. The use of the word "Baptist" as part of a name of a group happened in the sixteenth century on the heels of Luther's reformation.

The "Anabaptists" were "rebaptizers." They did not accept infant baptism and baptized only those who made a declaration of faith, thus rebaptizing some who had been baptized as infants. This approach put them in sharp opposition to both Roman Catholics and the new reform movements. Many Anabaptists were killed—often by drowning or burning at the stake. One of the best known was Balthasar Hubmaier, who was burned at the stake in Vienna; his wife was drowned.

A developer of Anabaptists in a more peaceful climate in the Netherlands was Menno Simons, founder of the Mennonites. John Smythe, a former clergyman in the Church of England, supported a Puritan Separatist (or break-off) movement, and had fled to Amsterdam. There he came into contact with the Mennonites. He organized his own congregation, with the practice of baptizing adults. History regards him as a bit unstable. Soon he broke off with the congregation. Thomas Helwys helped to lead a large part of that congregation to England where, in about 1612, he helped to form the first Baptist church in England.

Roger Williams was to do the same task in colonial America in 1639. He launched the first Baptist church along the lines that Helwys had followed.

Roger Williams grew up in London, the son of the owner of a tailor shop. Young Williams often helped his father. The Williams' house was near the prison, where there were continual public executions, many dying simply because their beliefs were different from those in authority. The boy Roger apparently saw many of these horrible events. The people would laugh and make fun of the condemned, but young Williams reacted with a sense of horror and pity. Perhaps this is the beginning of a main emphasis in his teachings—that there should be separation of church and state. He felt that people should be allowed to have different opinions and live by their consciences without fear of prison or death.

Roger Williams' mother had come from a prominent family, and the young man met some very important people, among them Sir Edward Coke, an open-minded lawyer and judge. When Coke was named chief justice in the king's court, he gave Roger a job keeping the notes on the happenings in the Court of the Star Chamber. This notorious court passed judgment on editors, religious dissenters—whoever disagreed with the authorities. Again, Williams became more determined than ever to fight for freedom of conscience some day.

Coke sponsored Williams at the Charterhouse School in London, which John Wesley was to attend in the next century, and also at Pembroke College at Cambridge.

Williams followed the leadership of Coke and sided with the Puritans, who opposed the formality of the Church of England and sought reforms for a simpler way of worship. Williams did graduate studies at Cambridge and mastered Latin, Greek, Hebrew, Dutch, and French. He served as a chaplain in a prominent home. There he met some future leaders, among them, Oliver Cromwell, who took over power in England after the execution of King Charles I.

Then suddenly Sir Edward Coke was arrested and sent to the notorious Tower of London by King James I. James, favoring the Church of England, had little regard for the Puritans. His successor, Charles I, dealt even more harshly with them. The king allowed the archbishop, William Laud, to follow a policy of cruelty to Puritan dissenters. When one Puritan had his ears cut off and face branded and was imprisoned for life, Williams threw his hat in with the Puritans and dissenters. He fired off a pamphlet, *Dissent*, to the archbishop. Predictably, Laud was angry. The archbishop ordered Williams to be brought to trial. Williams, who already had an invitation to preach at a Puritan church in Boston, secretly slipped aboard the first ship he could for America. He was twenty-eight and had great hopes for the new land.

But after Williams, with his wife, Mary, settled in Boston in the Massachusetts Bay Colony, he found the pioneers just as tyrannical as the king and archbishop in England. These New World Puritans were very strict and felt all who lived in their area should be forced to believe as they. When the Boston church, taking a liking to Williams, offered him the position of teacher and preacher, Williams surprised them and turned them down. He didn't want to be a part of an "unseparated" church.

Williams and his wife proceeded to go to other parts of the colony and settled with a group of open-minded persons in Salem. He also spent a good bit of time among the Narragansett Indians. He began to denounce the Massachusetts Bay Colony government for cheating the Indians out of their land.

Fearing arrest, Williams fled to Plymouth. But he soon found that Pilgrims in Plymouth also did not believe in separation of church and state. Williams went back to Salem. He pressed his battle with the authorities for freedom of conscience for all. He declared that there never was a government which held a sword over the church that ever did any good. He said this in a sermon, then published it for all to read.

The authorities were now determined to get rid of Williams and all like him. The General Court of the Colony in 1634 approved an oath that all would have to take. The oath said the state had full rule in religion and could punish any who did not sign the oath and accept the strict rules of the Puritans. Swearing, working on Sunday, not going to Puritan church services were all punishable. When Williams spoke out against the new oath, he was arrested and brought to trial.

Williams sat in court and listened to one after another read from his sermons his angry words in defense of freedom. Given a chance to speak at last, he answered all charges with words from the Scriptures. He said he accepted the Ten Commandments, but the commandments dealing with worshipping God and honoring him were not to be enforced by the state.

The leaders convicted him and gave him three weeks to leave the colony. He took ill. They gave him some more time. At last, when Williams heard they were going to put him on a boat to England, he fled. It was the dead of winter. He left behind, for the moment, his wife and baby, and in the midst of a terrible blizzard, he headed east toward his Narragansett Indian friends. The next day he reached one of their camps where he was warmly received.

During the winter, Williams decided that if he were going to live in a place where freedom of conscience was allowed, he would have to build such a place himself. He bought some land from the Indians for a village. He decided to call it Providence, in appreciation of "God's merciful providence" to him in his time of difficulty. He sent for his wife and child and friends.

Gradually the new little colony grew, and after three years Williams decided it was time to have a church. He had himself immersed in a cold stream by one of his followers, an Anabaptist who had been at the Salem church. Then Williams in turn baptized him. This was the beginning of the Providence Baptist Church, the first Baptist church in America.

A meetinghouse was built for the small congregation. But Williams was restless, as usual, and he stayed as pastor for only three or four months.

He went to England to get a charter for the colony from Parliament. While he was waiting, he wrote a pamphlet, *The Bloody Tenent of Persecution for Cause of Conscience*, about separation of church and state. Many in Parliament did not like it and had it burned by the public hangman. However, Williams had friends from earlier days who were now influential, and he received his charter for Rhode Island. He served as president, or governor, of the colony from 1654 to 1657.

Roger Williams kept close ties with the Narragansett Indians and produced a dictionary in their language. He died in Providence sometime in March 1684, at the age of eighty.

ECOMING A BAPTIST

Although Baptists have less "doctrine" and fewer practices than many churches, some Baptist churches have become more formal. Many Baptist clergy now wear some kind of robe in the pulpit. Some, such as the Reverend Dr. Walter Pulliam, pastor of the Judson Baptist Church in Minneapolis, and president for a two-year term of the American Baptist Churches in the U.S.A., wear a stole also—a scarflike garment patterned after the Jewish "tallith."

Baptists do not use any creeds or books of liturgies and services. On communion Sunday, once a month, many do read together a "covenant" placed in the back of the hymnal. The covenant, which is a pledge to worship, pray, and serve together, is not binding on or required of any members.

Over the years, Baptists have called strongly for the separation of church and state, as Roger Williams did. Traditionally, they have opposed things such as a government representative from the United States to the Vatican. Baptists, while they have national associations and agencies and meet in national conventions, leave authority to each local congregation, which alone owns the church property.

One becomes a Baptist by first professing, or declaring openly, a belief in Jesus as savior. A person becomes a member after baptism, which is by immersion, being put under the water. Thus from baptism, Baptists get their name.

Many Baptist churches today, like other denominations, will accept members from other churches who may have been baptized in different ways. Baptism is considered a sign of a faith and commitment, but provides no special grace or power on its own.

The same is true of the Lord's Supper and communion. The Lord's Supper, like baptism, is called an "ordinance," a rule or practice of faith. An ordinance is distinct from a sacrament, which brings a special blessing, grace, or significance on its own. At the Judson Baptist Church, a member of the American (Northern) Baptist Churches in the U.S.A., considered one of the more liberal Baptist denominations, there is room for variety and for impromptu approaches in the Lord's Supper.

At the outset of the Lord's Supper observance recently, Pastor Pulliam at the Judson Church told the congregation, "This is the Lord's table. We simply administer the elements, and all are invited to partake."

Then, at Dr. Pulliam's side, the Reverend Dee Dunn, not a member of the church staff, continued: "The bread is something common to most of our tables. We eat bread . . . nutrients that give us life. We come to the communion table which represents the body of Christ, and we are reminded today to invite Christ's life into our spiritual life to nurture us and feed us."

She proceeds to give trays with little pieces of whole-wheat bread to the men and women who today are servers. They distribute the bread pieces to the congregation. "Take, eat, allowing Christ to feed us," said Ms. Dunn.

Then, Dr. Pulliam, taking the trays of small glasses of grape juice and preparing to give the trays to the servers to take also to the congregation, said, "Here's that cup again." He was referring to the way Jesus had prayed in the garden for the symbolic cup of sorrow and death to pass by. But as Christ accepted it, so the pastor urged the acceptance of the symbolic cup or small glasses of wine (most Baptist churches use grape juice) and the responsibility in faith that it stood for. "Sometimes we don't want the cup," which, he said, stood for the "death of Jesus on the way to the fullness of life . . . a symbol for us as we participate today."

And then, as he handed the trays with the tiny filled glasses to the servers he said, "The invitation is so simple. . . . 'All of you, drink of it," quoting the words of Jesus in the New Testament.

MEET A YOUNG LADY WHO STEPPED INTO THE WATERS OF FAITH

Julie and her family sing hymns at Judson Church.

It was 10:10 on Easter morning. White lilies lined the chancel or front of the church.

The communion table that usually stood in front of a wood panel on the platform beneath the high choir loft had been moved to the side.

Suddenly, following the joyous opening Easter hymns, the wood

137

panel doors slid back. The pastor, Walter Pulliam, in white robes stood visible to the congregation only from the chest up. He was standing in a *baptistry*, a small roomlike tank of water. Julie Baldridge, eleven at the time, stood with five other young people in the wings.

When the pastor motioned to her, Julie, also in a white robe, came slowly down the stairs into the water, her head and shoulders in view of the congregation.

Her hands were clasped in prayer against her chest. She continued into the water.

Baptists believe that when Jesus went down into the water to be baptized by John the Baptist in the Jordan River, Jesus was immersed, that is, he went under the water. This act is symbolic of new commitment, and for followers of Jesus, symbolic of a new life and forgiveness or cleansing of sins. Some other churches sprinkle or dip water on the initiate, believing that this is what John did in Jesus' case—that the original Greek New Testament wording suggests that Jesus went into the water, but once there water was sprinkled on his head.

Now, as Julie Baldridge, who is of Cherokee Indian descent, comes into the water, Pastor Pulliam reaches to her and leads her to the center of the baptistry.

Baptists do not put any special store in the words that follow and so there are apt to be variations in the baptism formula. Many clergy pronounce words baptizing the person in the name of the Father, the Son, and Holy Spirit.

But Pastor Pulliam explained later, "We try not to use all the cliché formula statements. I may say it differently each time."

The pastor asked Julie, the candidate for baptism, if she believed in Jesus Christ as her savior. She said she did, an act of profession of faith before the congregation.

He took her gently by the shoulder, held her folded hands and leaned her back into the water, saying, "In the name of Christ, I baptize you."

As he lifted her back out of the water, he said, "Amen," an acknowledgement of an accomplished fact.

Then he led her to the other end of the baptistry pool and members of a reception committee received her and led her out of the water. She returned to a changing room, then put on her Easter clothes.

Later in the service, Julie and the other newly baptized persons were brought into the church to receive the "right hand of fellowship." The pastor shook their hands, saying a word of happy welcome. Now Julie was an official member of the church, with the right to vote and participate in the life of the congregation.

To prepare for baptism, she had gone to six separate class sessions. The classes she took that spring before Easter while in the sixth grade were: (1) a quick survey of the major religions; (2) a study of the Jewish roots of the faith; (3) the history of the church through the centuries, with attention to some Baptist personalities such as Roger Williams; (4) a study of the Judson Church's central stained-glass window—this "teaching window" has twenty scenes from the life of Jesus; (5) a look at the meaning of baptism; and (6) the organization of the local church.

Although baptism for Baptists is a symbol only, Julie believes she does feel closer to God and Jesus since baptism. After baptism, she said, "You become closer to God and talk to him more and understand him more." To her, "God is a friend who helps you and understands you." She says that's what her favorite Bible verse, John 3 : 16—"For God so loved the world, that he gave his only begotten Son," is all about.

God is also a Spirit, according to Julie, which is in keeping with her Native American heritage. Her great-grandparents were Cherokees in Oklahoma. Recently her father, who is a chaplain for the Greater Minneapolis Council of Churches, inherited a ceremonial headdress from a Cherokee uncle.

The Cherokees, Julie points out, are close to nature and respect life, and they believe in God as a Spirit. They have much in their heritage that could be learned by others. Julie is now thirteen and in the seventh grade at Minnetonka Junior High School in Minneapolis, nearly two years after that Easter she was baptized.

She is active in a Sunday school class, called the "Uppers," because it meets in an upper room above the church sanctuary or main auditorium.

They read scripture together, talk about the sermon (church service is before the Sunday school), and may even play a Bible trivia game. They take up some difficult subjects, as they did recently with a discussion of teen suicide. A young medical doctor, Dr. Greg Lehman, is teacher. Julie and other students heard how important it is to learn how to pick up signals of young people in trouble who are silently seeking help. "There are people reaching out, and you can be there," said Dr. Lehman.

Julie has a sister, Amy, nine. While Julie wears her hair pulled back and clasped with a silver and white bow, Amy prefers a braided ponytail. Amy sees her older sister as a friend. "She likes to play together with me," said Amy, and they have devised a library game with their books at home.

Julie likes to read romance novels and plays the flute in the band at school.

BRANCHES OF BAPTISTS

Like the Methodists and Presbyterians, the Baptists split between North and South in Civil War times. While the various Methodists and Presbyterians and others have finally healed the wounds from the Civil War era and merged to a large degree, the Baptists have not gotten together. Baptists pride themselves on being independent, an attitude which does not lend itself to mergers.

The *Southern Baptist Convention*, formed in 1845, the largest Protestant denomination in the country, is traditionally quite conservative and evangelical. This, in some periods of time, has meant more concern with the Bible and conversions than with social issues. The *American Baptist Church*, to which Julie Baldridge belongs, is likely to be more experimental. The deacons are in charge of the spiritual life of the church and serve communion. This office is rotated among the American (Northern) Baptists. Dr. Pulliam of the American Baptists no longer has deacons in his congregation but "commissioners," who serve on commissions and committees, and some of whom serve communion. Southern Baptists ordain deacons for life.

A key difference between the American (Northern) and the Southern Baptists is in organization. Southern Baptists are more centralized, with more power vested in national boards and societies than the less structured American Baptists.

The *National Baptist Convention of America* and *National Baptist Convention, U.S.A., Inc.*, are primarily black Baptists. Both groups are very large. The National Baptist Convention of America is the "unincorporated," more independent group, while the National Baptist Convention, U.S.A., Inc., is incorporated and centrally structured. There is a third, newer black Baptist group, the *Progressive National Baptist Convention, Inc.*

Members of the *American Baptist Association* believe the other groups have too much organization and that there should be no organization beyond the local congregation. They have been called "Church Equality Baptists" and are more conservative. They hold to the Bible literally and question some views of modern science.

Free Will Baptists hold the views of Arminius, a Dutch scholar (1560–1609). Arminius believed that Christ died for all and that a person comes to God by his own free will. Arminius believed many will be saved, in contrast to the Calvinists, who hold that a chosen few, already predestined, will be saved. Arminius also had an influence on Wesley and the Methodists.

The Free Will Baptists also have the rite of foot washing, and they anoint the sick with oil. Formerly, they were distinguished by practicing open communion—that is, any believer is invited to partake of communion in their churches. But now that doesn't seem unusual, as many Protestant churches with a growing interest in church unity follow this practice.

The *Seventh Day Baptist General Conference* is similar to other Baptists except for the insistence on keeping Saturday as the Sabbath. Seventh Day Baptists, tracing their origins back to the 1600s in England, have a reputation for open-mindedness and a desire to work together with other groups. Churches are independent, but they look for fellowship and guidance to a General Conference, which meets annually, and to a Seventh Day Baptist World Federation of conferences.

PENTECOSTALS

Jeanine Rubino and a friend take part in a church service.

"They shouted three days and three nights. It was the Easter season. The people came from everywhere. By the next morning there was no way of getting near the house. As the people came in they would fall under God's power; and the whole city was stirred. They shouted there until the foundation of the house gave way, but no one was hurt."

—Report on the Azusa Street, Los Angeles, meetings in 1906
as retold in the *Pentecost Evangel*

HE ONE-EYED PREACHER OF AZUSA STREET

He stood tall in the small home-church meeting on Bonnie Brae Street in Los Angeles and gave a sermon on what he felt strongly in his heart. W. J. Seymour was supposed to be the new pastor of the group—until he gave his sermon. He talked about speaking in tongues, the speaking in special languages by one filled with the Holy Spirit.

After all, in the Book of Acts in the Bible Peter and the Apostles were said to speak in exciting, strange languages as they felt the Holy Spirit come upon them.

But Seymour, as he preached, sensed that the members did not agree with him. They were to tell him he was going too far. Speaking in tongues was limited to Biblical times and seemed out of place today, they said. They told Seymour, the one-eyed, largely untrained preacher who had recently come from Texas, that they didn't want him as pastor after all.

Yet Seymour and that "Holiness" church group did agree that a "second baptism," a receiving of the power of the Holy Spirit, was very important. The experience results in "sanctification," or being "made holy" or perfect in the Christian life by the power of the Holy Spirit. Only, the Holiness churches did not take to talking in tongues or strange languages when moved in joy by the Holy Spirit. Speaking in tongues was to become one of the things that distinguished Pentecostal from Holiness churches.

The Pentecostals take their name from the Feast of Pentecost, which is roughly seven weeks or fifty days after Easter ("Pentecost" means "fiftieth"). It was on Pentecost that Peter and others first spoke in tongues.

In the Scriptures, Jesus had just ascended into heaven on Pentecost. "And there appeared to them tongues as of fire, distributed and resting on each one of them. And they were all filled with the Holy Spirit and began to speak in other tongues, as the Spirit gave them utterance" (Acts 2 : 2–4).

When Seymour was not asked back to the Holiness church group as speaker or as pastor, he went to lead Baptist services in a private home. Baptists traditionally do not speak in tongues. But in that little meeting of black and white Christians—Seymour was black—seven members began to speak in tongues. The day is remembered in American Pentecostal history—April 9, 1906.

Seymour, who had not experienced that particular happening before, received the tongue-speaking gift of the Spirit three days later.

It is said that one young woman, Jennie Moore, who later became

Seymour's wife, went over to a piano and sang beautifully in what was believed to be Hebrew.

The word got around that strange and wonderful things were happening at the house. Crowds began to come, and Seymour spoke to the interracial gathering from the porch.

Seymour moved his followers into an old deserted Methodist church building on Azusa Street. The people came and sat on planks laid over empty nail kegs. Seymour piled up two wooden crates for a pulpit for the meetings that lasted from ten o'clock in the morning to ten o'clock at night.

For three years the meetings continued daily. Waves of Pentecostalism washed like a tide across the United States and onto other continents.

By some estimates there are over two hundred Pentecostal denominations. The largest and one of the best known is the Assemblies of God.

B ECOMING A MEMBER OF THE ASSEMBLIES OF GOD

Most churches have several steps, such as baptism, confirmation, or first communion, as one comes to share in the full life of the church. Assemblies of God and other Pentecostals have their steps as well, but their approach is different.

Pentecostals first believe in Christ as a personal savior—usually accompanied by baptism in water near the time of the decision. Then, with prayer, one receives the Holy Spirit, a "second blessing." Some Pentecostals say the gift of speaking in tongues comes at the time of the receiving of the Holy Spirit. This is what the Assemblies of God believe, and this "two-step" approach is called the "two experiences" of grace. Some Pentecostals say there are really three steps or experiences: belief, baptism of the Holy Spirit (with sanctification or purifying of one's life), and then the third experience of speaking in tongues.

Pentecostals and those in the Assemblies of God are baptized by immersion or dipping in water, as an "outward sign" of the working of God and the changing of heart. Like the Baptists and others, baptism comes usually when one is old enough to feel and understand a faith in Jesus and know that sins are forgiven. The second baptism of the Spirit may come at any time. A person may be drawn to a special prayer group after a church service, either in front of the pulpit or in a side room. As a person kneels in intense prayer with others, often with a church leader, the feeling of the

Spirit comes in a rush of joy and enthusiasm—and then comes the speaking in tongues.

Once a person has experienced the presence and gifts of the Spirit, there are various ways in which he or she might behave. The Grace Church of Kendall (Assemblies of God) in Miami suggests in a little brochure with drawings these ways of behaving when one is filled with the Spirit at a service of the church or in prayer: (1) speaking in tongues (Acts 2 : 4; 1 Corinthians 14); (2) interpreting and explaining the meaning of talking in tongues (1 Corinthians 12 and 14); (3) being "slain in the Spirit," in which one falls and remains motionless for a while under the influence of the Spirit (Matthew 28 : 4; Acts 9 : 4); (4) laying of hands on a person and anointing with a spot of oil (Mark 16 : 18; Acts 9 : 17; James 5 : 14); (5) presenting a special word of knowledge or understanding for others to hear (1 Corinthians 12 : 8); (6) lifting up hands in praise (Psalms 63 : 4; 1 Timothy 2 : 8) and (7) singing in the Spirit (Psalm 33 : 3; 1 Corinthians 14 : 15), creating a new song in praise.

The Assemblies of God may dedicate babies but save baptism, often referred to as baptism of repentance, for those who have expressed their faith in Jesus. The Lord's Supper with communion is an act of "remembrance," remembering the Lord's death (1 Corinthians 11 : 26). A third rite or ordinance is the washing of the feet of the faithful, an act of humility recalling Jesus' own washing of the feet of the disciples.

Assemblies of God members believe in healing through prayer as one of the gifts of the Spirit. "Testimonies," personal stories of faith and answered prayer, are part of the church life. Members believe in the second coming of Jesus, followed by a one-thousand-year reign of Jesus on earth. Most believe they are living in the last days before the coming of Jesus and cite the disasters and sin and troubles in the world as examples of the nearing end. They are democratic, with the authority of the church in the hands of the local congregation. There is very little difference between a pastor and a church member. In fact, the people are likely to call the leader "brother" or "sister" instead of "pastor" or "reverend."

MEET A YOUNG LADY IN THE SPIRIT

Jeanine and a friend study in Sunday school class.

Jeanine Rubino, thirteen, had always wondered what it would be like to be really bowled over by the Spirit—"slain by the Spirit," as some call it, when the Holy Spirit takes over like a bolt of electricity.

Jeanine, an eighth grader at the Arvida Junior High School in Miami and member of Grace Assembly of God Church, found out one summer at camp in Winter Haven, Florida.

The young member of the Assemblies of God denomination was in prayer following a stirring sermon by a youth pastor. "A group of us were still involved in prayer after the sermon," said the dark-haired, dark-eyed young lady in an interview in her church in the Kendall district on Miami's southwest side. "The pastor told us who were praying to go into a separate room."

The pastor came and talked to the young people, and Jeanine remembers he said, "Let it go, just let it go. Just say 'I love you Jesus,' and it can happen." And they did. "We said it over and over."

The quiet all-A student recalls, "It was a weird sensation for me . . . exciting. Unknown tongues came to me naturally. . . ."

The Spirit gave her words and special sounds, which came out very fast. She says she was not conscious of speaking any special language, but the words had a sense of joy that let her empty her soul in praise of God.

The experience is also physical, Jeanine says. "So many that day at the camp were 'slain' in the Spirit," falling backwards on the floor or shaking.

She has yet to be baptized with water, a symbolic act of commitment to Christ that usually comes first. However, the "second" baptism of the Spirit's bringing power can come anytime to the believer. Jeanine plans to be baptized soon. The pastor of Grace Church, the Reverend John Alessi, will immerse her in water before the congregation.

A partition panel comes away behind the pulpit. In white robe, symbolic of new life and purity, Jeanine will be standing in water up to her waist. Pastor Alessi will let her down into the water and then up and will say that he is baptizing her in the name of the Father and of the Son and of the Holy Spirit. She may be invited to give her testimony, words about what her faith means to her, at this time or shortly afterwards.

Jeanine may become a missionary some day, but right now she thinks her first choice will be to become a fashion designer and editor. She stands straight, quietly, but bearing confidence. With her dark eyes and dark hair in a smart black-and-white plaid dress, she, indeed, does look as if she stepped right out of a fashion ad.

She is the fashion writer for her school paper, *The Viking*. She likes volleyball and other sports. She holds a presidential physical fitness award and has a first-place ribbon for the 600-yard race during the school field day.

Jeanine is described by parents and friends as shy, but forward when she has something to say. Her mother is church secretary. Her father is a carpenter and an usher at the church. He says Jeanine is "at an age where she knows she will have eternal life and she has a peace of mind because of her faith."

Steve Alessi, a youth pastor and soloist at the church, says Jeanine is "very mature spiritually and knows in what direction she wants to go. She's a quiet leader who can always get the other girls to bake cookies or help in some way." She sets an example, but softly, he adds. He told of the time some of the girls she was staying with at a youth camp turned on inappropriate adult fare on TV. "She just quietly left the room," he said hc was told. "She's bold in her faith, not pushy, and kids respect her."

Each week she gives a tithe of fifty cents—10 percent of her five dollars allowance—to the church.

During the church service at Grace Church she sits with her friends. The service reaches peak moments when people are saying "amen" and "halleluia" and other responses as they are caught up in the great anthems of the church. These are accompanied by organ, drums, trombones, and trumpets. Soon some are standing in the congregation, happy in the Spirit, waving their arms and swaying. Jeanine is clapping, as are others who are not standing. It is a moment of beauty and joy as the faithful feel the power of the Spirit through faith.

Praying and receiving the Holy Spirit at a conference on the Holy Spirit in Jerusalem.

A visiting preacher gives the sermon and talks about the power of the Spirit to bring miracles. He tells about the time Jesus walked on water and bid Peter to follow him from the boat (Matthew 14 : 22–33). The preacher tells of the timidity of those who stayed in the boat, while Peter ventured out. "Step out of the boat into miracles," he declares, as he preaches, walking at times away from the pulpit. Several times during the service there are prayers for healing. At one moment, those who wish healing for any ailment or who simply have feelings of "hurt" come forward to the front of the church. Leaders of the church anoint, or touch, their heads with oil and then they move on to join others at the front of the church for prayers of healing.

Jeanine once went forward with her mother for prayers of healing, she explained. She had just started junior high school, "and I had a lot of anxiety," she said. The laying of hands on her forehead and the prayers that followed, she recalls, helped a lot and relieved her anxiety.

Up front, a large round stained-glass window featuring a dove descending is the center of attention in the design of the church. It symbolizes the descending of the Spirit in the form of a dove at the baptism of Jesus (Matthew 3 : 16).

When Jeanine takes communion in the church, she goes to the front and takes a piece of bread from a common loaf. Also she takes the wine in a little glass. Returning to her pew with the bread and wine, she and the congregation eat and drink together, recalling the death of Jesus for them and the forgiveness of sins.

Before the church service is an hour of Sunday school. Waiting for it to begin, Jeanine chats with her friends, who somehow have learned that her recent report card had all As.

Soon the teacher, Kathy Adderley, who teaches at Miami's Killian Senior High during the week, begins the study. The day's theme is the story of the ten maidens who took their lamps to greet the bridegroom (Matthew 25 : 1–13). Five were foolish and took no oil with them for the lamps; five were prepared. While the five foolish ones were off buying the oil, the bridegroom came, and the five foolish ones missed the occasion. The parable closes with, "Watch therefore, for you know neither the day nor the hour wherein the Son of Man comes."

The students, including Jeanine, takes turns reading Bible verses and learn, as Ms. Adderley impresses on them, that nobody knows when Christ is to return. They can only be ready for his return at all times.

"Would it be fair," she said, "if one treats his fellow man as horribly as he can, parties all night, and hears just in time that Jesus is to return that morning, then gets back in time for a little rest to show up for his return? No, that's not fair," she said. No one, indeed, knows the time and one must be ready all the time, she explained.

"Can I depend on all of you to stay in the word this week and pray for one another?" she concluded. Jeanine was called on for a final moment of prayer. She thanked God for his word and prayed for strength to be prepared.

BRANCHES OF PENTECOSTALISM

The Pentecostal kind of churches cover a wide range. Some keep the word "Holiness" or have "Apostolic" or "Church of God" or "Foursquare Gospel" in their names. Several of these will be mentioned later in the book. Here are descriptions of some that have "Pentecostal" in their titles.

Basically similar to the Assemblies of God, the *Pentecostal Church of Zion* places more emphasis on the Old Testament. They keep Saturday as the Sabbath and follow Mosaic law in the Old Testament, forbidding the eating of pork, plus other restrictions.

One of the controversies in Pentecostal history was whether a person should be baptized with water in the name of the Trinity (Father, Son, and Holy Spirit) or only in the name of Jesus. This "Jesus only" group the *United Pentecostal Church*, upholds the "oneness" of God (a term that describes the movement) rather than the Trinity. They believe that Jesus represents God and baptism should be in his name only (Acts 2 : 38). This group has a strict living code. For example: Women do not cut their hair; members have no TV sets; boys and girls may not swim together.

Similar to the United Pentecostal Church, the *Pentecostal Assemblies of the World* also believes that for salvation one must become holy and remain holy for the rest of his or her life. There are strict rules for daily life. The group is also pacifist, and declines to take part in war.

Much of Pentecostalism has a Methodist as well as Baptist heritage and the *Pentecostal Holiness Church* reflects the Methodist form of organization. Like the Methodists, this church has an overall general conference every four years to set policies. The general conference elects two superintendents (like bishops) for four-year terms. These are "three-step" Pentecostals—acceptance of Jesus (justification by faith), sanctification (purification by the Spirit), and the Spirit baptism into speaking in tongues.

Amish boys, dressed in "plain clothes" enjoying ice cream.

152

OTHER GROUPS

AMISH

OLD ORDER AMISH MENNONITE CHURCH

You have seen pictures of the Amish and their children—the men and boys with broad-brimmed hats and beards; the women in bonnets and aprons. As they drive about in their horse-drawn buggies in Eastern Pennsylvania and in other states, they look as if they are from another era. And indeed, that's the way they want it.

The Amish and the "Old Order" come out of a Mennonite tradition (see "Mennonites"; also Chapter 12 on *Baptists).* They are named after their seventeenth-century leader, Jacob Amman, a French-Swiss Mennonite bishop who believed in following the Bible literally in utmost simplicity.

Amman preached the practice of "avoidance." This is placing under a ban, or avoiding, any member of their group who goes astray. In fact, they are to avoid society as far as possible. Even schooling, beyond the three Rs—"reading, 'riting, and 'rithmetic"—is discouraged. Worship services are held in members' homes on a rotating basis. Ministers are chosen by lot from a group of nominees.

ARMENIAN APOSTOLIC CHURCH

DIOCESE OF THE ARMENIAN CHURCH OF AMERICA

Tradition has it that two of Jesus' disciples, Thaddeus and Bartholomew, went north to preach in the foothills of Mount Ararat, where tradition says Noah's ark landed in Armenia, now a part of the Soviet Union, next to Turkey. Ancient Armenia is now divided between Turkey, the Soviet Union, and Iran. The Holy See, or spiritual center of the Armenian Apostolic church, is in Etchmiadzin in Soviet Armenia, one of the fifteen republics of the Soviet Union. Some, such as the *Armenian Apostolic Church of America*, relate also to Antelias, near Beirut, Lebanon, and the "catholicos," or universal leader, there.

The Armenian Apostolic Church in 451 A.D. could not take part in the Council of Chalcedon (near Constantinople) which affirmed that Christ had two natures, divine and human. Certain Eastern Christians, such as the Armenians, preferred the earlier Council of Ephesus in 431 A.D., which said that Christ had "one nature united in the incarnate Word," that is, Jesus. The emphasis on "one nature" preserved the "mystery" of Christ's incarnation, the Armenians argued. The Armenian Apostolic Church is sometimes referred to as "monophysite," literally, "one nature."

Jason Kaloustian, fifteen, of Visalia, California, is a member of St. Mary Armenian Orthodox Church and serves as a stole bearer at the altar. He points to the fact that Armenia became a Christian nation in 301 A.D., more than a decade before Constantine won his battle that led to making Christianity the official religion of the Roman Empire.

Jason, who was baptized and confirmed at three months, says, "My religion helps me to become a stronger person, knowing that the belief of my forefathers through the centuries has not changed and is continuing to grow."

B AHA'I FAITH

Two persons are prominent in the launching of the Baha'i Faith. One is Mirza Ali Muhammad, known as the Bab ("The Gate"), a descendant of Muhammad. In 1844 he announced in Shiraz, Persia, that he was to foretell the coming of a long-sought special messenger of God, a role similar to that of John the Baptist proclaiming the advent of Christ.

The Bab was martyred in Tabriz, Persia, and a young man, Mirza Husayn'Ali, who took the name of Baha'u'llah ("Glory of God"), came forward to declare that he was the promised one. From Baha'u'llah the Baha'is get their name. To Baha'is, the Bab and Baha'u'llah are considered cofounders of the faith. Before his death in 1892, Baha'u'llah spent much of his life in prison for his beliefs.

Baha'is believe God is the creator of all and that a sense of unity of mankind must develop. There are no clergy, no initiation ceremonies or sacraments. Membership is open to any who accept Baha'u'llah as God's latest prophet and wish to follow his teachings. Baha'is pray daily and meet in local gatherings called "feasts" every nineteen days.

Carla Michelle Pleasant, sixteen, of Little Rock, Arkansas, became a member of the Baha'is on her fifteenth birthday, when she signed a membership card "indicating my belief in Baha'u'llah as the latest messenger of God for this day."

A tap dancer and violin player, she teaches a Sunday school class and takes part in the informal evening discussions called "firesides," where questions are answered and the faith is discussed.

"The Baha'i Faith is progressive," she says. "We learn about a new manifestation for today. The Baha'i Faith brings about unity, which is really important for the nations and the world. You open up your eyes and see something new, something now. The Baha'i Faith means agreement of all religions, bringing peace on earth."

B RETHREN

CHURCH OF THE BRETHREN

Regarded as a historic peace church, the Church of the Brethren is pacifist—members do not fight in war. They do not take oaths. Some do not take part in lawsuits. However, the church is known for its relief projects to famine victims and others in need and for its strong positive education program for peace.

The Brethren strive to live a simple life, practice temperance, and shun modern amusements. Baptism is by immersion—three times in succession in the name of each of the three members of the Trinity.

Originally exiles from persecution in Germany, the Brethren came to America in 1719 to settle on free lands provided by William Penn in the Philadelphia area.

C HRISTIAN AND MISSIONARY ALLIANCE

Two organizations—the Christian Alliance, which sought to deepen the meaning of faith, and the Evangelical Missionary Alliance, which sent out missionaries, merged in 1887 to form the Christian and Missionary Alliance.

Members follow what is known as the "fourfold" Gospel formula. Christ is savior. He makes a person holy. He heals, and he is to come again and reign one thousand years before the end of the world. An annual General Council elects a board of managers. There are no highly paid officials. Each church is independent and self-supporting and sends out missionaries on its own.

CHRISTIAN SCIENCE

CHURCH OF CHRIST, SCIENTIST

Healing is very important in Christian Science. The church began with Mary Baker Eddy, who reportedly recovered from an injury in 1866 after reading about Jesus' healing of a man with palsy (paralysis) (Matthew 9 : 1–8). She had been a member of the Congregational church until she was over forty, but she had a growing sense of the power of God in healing sickness as well as in overcoming sin.

Mrs. Eddy saw spiritual healing as scientific, because it was provable and available for all. Christian Science describes God as a Divine Principle, or Mind, which is made known through the Master, or Way-shower, Jesus. They emphasize that man is created, as the Bible says, in the image of God and reflects Mind. All sin, suffering, and death are unreal. God, who created everything, said Mrs. Eddy, created only that which is good.

Jesus himself was more than just a good man. He was also the living example of man's oneness with God and showed through his teaching and life what it is to live a life with God.

The First Church of Christ, Scientist, in Boston, Massachusetts, and each of the worldwide branches elects a Board of Directors to do the work following the rules laid down in the *Manual of the Mother Church* by Mrs. Eddy.

The church has no ordained clergy. A Board of Directors associated with The Mother Church, The First Church of Christ, Scientist in Boston, directs the work of branch churches around the world, as specified by the *Manual*. A Board of Lectureship provides visiting lecturers to the churches. Each church has two readers, usually a man and a woman, who take turns reading from the Bible and Mrs. Eddy's book, *Science and Health with Key to the Scriptures*. The "lesson-sermon" is prepared in advance by a special committee of the Mother Church.

A midweek meeting includes testimonies of healing. Practitioners selected by the Board of Directors practice healing full-time. Christian Scientists place their faith in spiritual healing.

"I like the freedom of not taking medicine and of not being a slave to my body," says Chloe Berta, thirteen, a member of the First Church of Christ, Scientist at the Mother Church in Boston.

A budding artist and ardent water skier, she adds, "Also I like the way I think differently. When I pray about something, I discover so many new things, and that gives me a good feeling about my religion.

"Christian Science teaches me how to think about myself— what I am and who I am. It helps me understand more about God. He's sort of like the director and producer of the world, of people's actions, of everything. But we have to listen to him to learn more."

 # HURCH OF GOD

CHURCH OF GOD (ANDERSON, INDIANA)

Some two hundred church bodies use the name Church of God. And some are distinguished by the names of the cities where they have their headquarters. Five have their headquarters in Cleveland, Tennessee, and one is called *Church of God (Cleveland Tennessee)*. One of the largest is the denomination with headquarters in Anderson, Indiana.

Similar to Pentecostal churches, Church of God denominations believe that one is saved by faith alone. They believe there is a sanctification, or perfecting experience, and a baptism by the Holy Spirit, bringing the gifts of healing and speaking in tongues.

The Church of God in Anderson, Indiana, has baptism by immersion, the Lord's Supper, and foot-washing. The church emphasizes the unity of all Christians through shared spiritual experiences and not through shared creeds or doctrines.

 # HURCH OF GOD IN CHRIST

Started in Jackson, Mississippi, in 1894, by C. H. Mason, this predominantly black denomination is also closely associated with Pentecostal teaching. Mason, in fact, went out to the Azusa Street meetings, a source of the Pentecostal movement, in Los Angeles and was baptized there (see *Pentecostals*, Chapter 13). The group believes in the holiness experiences, spiritual healing, and the return of Christ to rule for one thousand years. The church is administered by a once-in-four-years General Assembly and a General Board of twelve presided over by a senior bishop.

OPTICS

Very similar in basic beliefs to the Greek Orthodox, the Coptics differ in that they, like the Armenian Apostolic Church, are monophysites, that is, they believe Christ had basically "one nature," uniting the human and divine. "Coptic" is an ancient word for "Egyptian," and this is basically an Egyptian church.

The church has a patriarch, also referred to as a pope, elected by the bishops. Only monks, those who live a simple life set off in monasteries, can be elected bishop. The church had been cut off from the rest of the world for so many centuries by Muslim rule that it has changed little. Its rituals are considered among the most ancient in Christianity.

 ISCIPLES OF CHRIST

CHRISTIAN CHURCH (DISCIPLES OF CHRIST)

Two groups that started as "revival" outdoor preaching movements at the beginning of the nineteenth century came together in 1832. They both sought to get back to the simple beliefs of New Testament times and felt that creeds and other traditional statements were not needed.

One group was the Disciples of Christ, launched by a former Presbyterian minister, Thomas Campbell, and his son, Alexander, in Western Pennsylvania. The other was the Christian Church, or Church of Christ, launched by Barton Stone, also a Presbyterian minister, in Kentucky.

The two groups joining together struggled with a name and decided on both: "Christian Church (Disciples of Christ)". Very similar to Baptists, the Disciples have two ordinances. Baptism by immersion for believers perhaps has a greater emphasis as a divine requirement than in the Baptist churches. Yet baptism is not done until after the person has been received into membership in the church. The Lord's Supper, administered with the aid of lay persons, is a memorial, or remembrance, of Christ's death and sacrifice. Participation in the Lord's Supper is open to any Christian. A general assembly of the denomination, with representatives from congregations, meets every two years.

JEHOVAH'S WITNESSES

The Hebrew word for God, *Yahweh*, or *Jehovah*, as the word for God is written at times in the King James Version of the Scriptures, appears 6,961 times in the Bible, Jehovah's Witnesses point out. They quote Psalm 83 : 18: "That men may know that you, whose name alone is Jehovah, are the most high over all the earth."

The "Witnesses" term comes from Isaiah 43 : 10–11 in the American Standard Version of the Bible: "You are my witnesses, says Jehovah, and my servant whom I have chosen; that you may know and believe me, and understand that I am he: before me there was no God formed, neither shall there be after me. I, even I, am Jehovah, and besides me there is no saviour."

The group had its beginnings in a Bible study group in the 1870s in Allegheny City, now a part of Pittsburgh, Pennsylvania. Charles Taze Russell was the leader and published a magazine, *Zion's Watch Tower and Herald of Christ's Presence*. A Zion's Watch Tower Tract Society was formed in 1884, with Russell as president.

Russell believed that the return of Christ was coming soon. When Russell died in 1916, Joseph F. Rutherford, a former Missouri lawyer and circuit court judge, became leader. The group was not actually called Jehovah's Witnesses until 1931. In 1939, the official name of the organization as it is today became The Watch Tower Bible and Tract Society, with headquarters in Brooklyn, New York.

Witnesses believe in a final battle of Armageddon. The name comes from the Hebrew for "mountain" and the plain of "Megiddo" in Israel where the battle is to be fought. In the battle, Christ and his angels will overpower Satan and his army. The believers will remain on earth, joined with the resurrected faithful. A new, cleansed earth will be ruled by the righteous. There is no hell as such. The wicked will be forever destroyed.

Some views of the Witnesses have caused controversies. They do not believe in taking blood into the body, either by eating or blood transfusions (Genesis 9 : 3–4; Leviticus 17 : 14; Acts 15 : 28–29). Believing in the rule of God, they do not take part in worldly government affairs and do not salute the flag or bear arms in war.

Their churches are called Kingdom Halls. Every member is a minister. They have well-planned rallies in cities across the United States. One in New York City drew a quarter of a million people.

Young people among Jehovah's Witnesses have responsibilities. Duane Gooding, sixteen, of Homer, Alaska, at his Kingdom Hall gives five-minute speeches, leads prayers, conducts Bible studies, and reads from publications. He also helps with the microphones for others taking part.

He was baptized (immersed) upon dedicating his life to "the true God Jehovah." Duane, who likes fishing and has won art honors at school, says he is happy that "the only true God Jehovah is giving me the chance to represent him, by telling others about him and his soon-to-come kingdom that will turn the whole earth into a paradise. Only those wanting to seek Jehovah will be able to live in this paradise, where no illness, death, crime, or imperfection that is experienced today will occur."

Brad Stitzel, fifteen, who likes skiing and skate-boarding, is the only teen Jehovah's Witness in his small Alaskan town of Valdez. He says, "My religion means faith and endurance, an everlasting stand, and gives me a true inner sense and security." Because Bible verses back up every belief, he says, "I can believe in my religion wholeheartedly without a doubt."

MENNONITES

MENNONITE CHURCH

Menno Simons, a former priest, became a leader of a group of Anabaptists, or rebaptizers, in Holland in the 1550s. Soon the movement was known by his name. The Mennonites reject infant baptism, accepting only baptism on the profession of faith. They were persecuted in various countries, but found a safe place in Germantown, near Philadelphia, on land provided by William Penn. The largest group is the Mennonite church, which holds a general assembly every two years with its bishops and local clergy and lay delegates.

Mennonites do not take public oaths, decline to fight in war, and do not take part in secret groups. The Lord's Supper is administered twice a year. Foot-washing is also practiced. They are noted for their charitable work and especially for a worldwide relief organization.

A young Mennonite in Kitchener, Ontario, Canada, Michelle E. A. Warren, fifteen, a cross-country runner, says she became a member of the Mennonites in May 1987 through water baptism by pouring. She likes most about her religion the "friendships and fellowship" and a youth program where the young person spends time with an adult friend. She wants to "grow and learn more" and "serve" and "share with those who can't help themselves."

MORAVIANS

MORAVIAN CHURCH IN AMERICA

Count Nicolaus Ludwig Graf von Zinzendorf was interested in a deepening spiritual life, or what he called "heart religion." In the 1720s he took in a group of refugees from recent wars in Europe and allowed them to found a village on his estate in the Austrian province of Moravia, now a part of Czechoslavakia.

Zinzendorf saw the group as a body of "soldiers" for Christ and organized them into a strict community almost like a monastery. Young men and women were allowed to marry but generally lived separately, with their children brought up apart from them. Zinzendorf saw the group as a "warm" spiritual fellowship within Lutheranism, but soon met much opposition. Many of the group came to the United States and settled in Georgia, Pennsylvania, and North Carolina.

Infants are baptized and full membership comes later at confirmation. The Lord's Supper is held six times a year. A governing provincial synod made up of ministers and lay persons meets every five years.

MORMONS

CHURCH OF JESUS CHRIST OF THE LATTER-DAY SAINTS

Joseph Smith, in Fayette, New York, learned in a vision from an angel of the existence of ancient metal plates or tablets of writing that would be shown to him. In 1827, at Hill Cumorah, near Manchester Village, New York, Smith received the plates of the Book of Mormon—an account by several Christian prophets. They told of ancient American people—among them the Jaredites, originally from the area of the Tower of Babel in ancient Babylon and the descendants of a dispersed tribe of ancient Israelites. The Jaredites are regarded by Mormons as forerunners of the American Indians.

Smith's translation of the golden plates became the *Book of Mormon*, a basic book of scripture, named for the prophet who compiled the records. Members of the church consider it complementary to the Bible, which they also use. In other visions, Smith and Oliver Cowdery received instructions and authority from John the Baptist, St. Peter, St. James, and St. John. Smith and Cowdery baptized each other, as instructed by John the Baptist.

The new church was persecuted from state to state as the members moved west to Ohio, then Missouri and Illinois. Joseph Smith himself and another leader, his brother Hyrum Smith, were killed in 1844 by a mob that stormed a Carthage, Illinois, jail where they were held.

Brigham Young was chosen Smith's successor and led the group west to the Salt Lake valley in what became the state of Utah. Salt Lake City is now the headquarters of the church. A prominent university was named after Young in nearby Provo, Utah, Brigham Young University, which, incidentally, had the number one college football team in the nation in 1984 and is the largest church-operated university in the country.

Mormons believe in the three persons of the Trinity. God the Father is described as a perfected personage of flesh and bones, a kind of man who, Joseph Smith said, "was once as we are now," but who became all-powerful, all-knowing. Jesus is seen as the literal Son of God, the Savior of all mankind. The Holy Ghost is viewed as a spirit person without a physical body.

Mormons have baptism by immersion. They observe the Lord's Supper every Sunday, using water, usually in paper cups. They lay on hands to pass on the gifts of the Holy Spirit, among them speaking in tongues and healing. They expect that Jesus, who they believe visited North America after his resurrection, will return to rule the earth.

All revelation may not be in the Bible or *Book of Mormon*, but may also occur through modern-day prophets, apostles, and teachers.

Mormons believe also in baptizing in behalf of the dead, namely those who may not have had a chance to hear the gospel. Keeping family history records and tracing the names of long-lost ancestors are important. Baptism does not alone save the dead, for in some way the dead have to themselves accept the faith. Baptism for the dead is performed with a living person as a stand-in for the dead person.

At the head of the Mormon organization is the First Presidency, which includes a president and two counselors; then there is a Council of the Twelve Apostles and other leaders in Salt Lake City. There are regional groupings called "stakes," with a president, counselors, and other officers. Congregations are called "wards," each presided over by a bishop and two counselors.

A young Mormon, Kirk Wynn Geis, fourteen, of Decatur, Alabama, who has a superior rating in his school band competition, was baptized at age eight, which Mormons consider the age of accountability. Says Kirk: "The baptism, which is not only physical but is for the remission of our sins, is a sacred covenant with our Father in heaven."

His religion means a lot to him, he says, "because, through the crucifixion of Jesus Christ and the resurrection of him, I can live with our heavenly Father again; also, to live with him we have to be baptized by immersion by those in authority. After I was baptized I have to live the true principles and ordinances of my religion."

At the age of twelve, he was ordained a deacon in the Aaronic priesthood (Aaron was the priestly brother of Moses). Adds Kirk: "The responsibilities that come with this are passing the sacrament [communion] and collecting fast offerings [donations to the poor and needy]. At the age of fourteen I was ordained to the priesthood office of a teacher. As teacher I received the responsibility to prepare the sacrament, and all the duties of deacon and teacher, which is to warn, exhort, to teach, and invite all to come to Christ."

N AZARENES

CHURCH OF THE NAZARENE

Formed as a merger of three "holiness" groups in 1908, this denomination was known first as the Pentecostal Church of the Nazarene. But about ten years later, "Pentecostal" was dropped from the name, partly to make it different from the Pentecostal groups that spoke in tongues, a practice in which the Nazarenes did not engage. However, the experience of "sanctification," the feeling of being made holy and spiritual by the Holy Spirit, remained, for the Nazarenes, a "second work of grace," beyond the experience of salvation.

Members believe in spiritual healing of the sick, but do not oppose going to doctors and hospitals. Nazarenes have two ordinances—baptism (by pouring, sprinkling, or immersion) and the Lord's Supper. Nazarenes have a general assembly which elects general superintendents for four-year terms.

QUAKERS

FRIENDS UNITED MEETING

George Fox (1624–1691) in England was a kind of "seeker" of faith who somehow did not find the faith and inner peace he was looking for in the main churches. He wrote, after he had given up hope for direction in the churches: "I heard a voice which said, 'There is one, even Christ Jesus, that can speak to thy condition.'" Fox identified this as an inner voice or an inner light that others could also have. He felt that Christianity is not just an outward profession of faith or practices on Sunday, but rather offered an inner light by which Christ lights the soul of the believer and moves a person on into service.

Followers of Fox had many names, among them, "Children of Truth" and "Friends of Truth." "Friends" is still the official name in the title of the groups today.

Fox spent some time in prison for his beliefs, and his followers were severely persecuted. Four were hanged for their beliefs in Massachusetts, for instance. In one court, Fox told the judge to "tremble at the Word of the Lord!" The judge in jest called him a "Quaker," and the name stuck.

George Fox, founder of the Society of Friends.

William Penn, himself a Quaker, received a land grant from Charles II and brought many Quaker refugees to America to settle in today's Pennsylvania.

Friends do not take oaths and are opposed to fighting in a war. They do not observe sacraments as such. They believe in baptism by the Spirit of God, but without using water. In many churches there is a long period of silence in which worshippers "wait" for God to speak within, to individuals and to the group. This is considered communion.

The Friends United Meeting is composed of seventeen yearly meetings, or groups, and seeks to coordinate Quaker mission and education work. It has a peace emphasis.

Peter Silver, sixteen, of Richmond, Indiana, who likes astronomy and kite flying, has been a Quaker from the time he was very young. "Quakers don't have baptism or anything," he says, "so there is no exact time I became one."

Being a Quaker, he says, means to him "trying to get in touch with that part of God that I think is inside me and to listen to it and to follow it and share that experience with other people."

He also likes "the lack of ritualistic trappings in Quakerism." He says, "Often other religions tend to obscure their basic tenets in ceremonies and hierarchies and special rules. The mode of worship in Quakerism is very simple and clear and everyone is pretty equal. My other favorite thing about Quakerism is the peace testimony."

REFORMED CHURCH IN AMERICA

The Reformed churches date back to the Reformation. They are linked to John Calvin in Geneva, Switzerland. Calvin's followers who went to Scotland became the nucleus of the Presbyterians; his followers who went to Holland became the Dutch Reformed Church. Dutch settlers launched the Reformed Protestant Dutch Church in the colonies in 1628, the oldest denomination in the nation. The name was changed to Reformed Church in America in 1867.

Worship in the Reformed Church in America is partly formal, but allows considerable freedom. Only the rituals for baptism and the Lord's Supper are spelled out. Each local church is run by a *consistory*, which is made up of elders who guide the spiritual life, deacons in charge of the stewardship and giving.

A young member of the denomination, Daniel Swart, fifteen, of

Sheboygan, Wisconsin, who likes computer programming, says he was baptized shortly after birth. "When I was thirteen," he says, "I made a confession of faith, which is an agreement between God and myself.

"Being a part of my religion means that I believe that Jesus is completely God and completely human and that he died on a cross to save all people. He had to be totally God to take away the sins of people, and he had to be totally human to take away the wrath of God.

"The first duty of a person in my religion is to love God and believe that he sent his Son, Jesus Christ, to die on the cross to save us. Because of this we are called to be obedient to him."

SALVATION ARMY

William Booth, a Methodist minister in England in the last century, wasn't happy with the formal ways that had developed in the churches. He withdrew and began traveling and preaching at revivals or religious gatherings around England. In 1865, he held meetings in London's east end slum in a tent in a Quaker graveyard. There were many converts.

Since neither Booth nor the newly converted felt at home in the churches, he set up Christian Mission Centers. Within two years he was joined by ten full-time workers and many volunteers.

The movement was militant and enthusiastic. Followers carried banners down the streets with the name, "The Christian Mission." Booth, reading a report on the movement, noticed someone had called it a "volunteer army." He penciled out the word "volunteer" and wrote in "salvation" and the Salvation Army was born.

Booth was the "general"; the mission centers, the "corps"; members were "soldiers," and ministers had officer ranks. Soon there were uniforms and a brass band.

Over the years the Army has concentrated on serving the needy and homeless. Its beliefs are set forth in its Foundation Deed document of 1878. The Bible is regarded as the rule of life; there is belief in the Trinity; salvation is through belief in Christ; and sanctification sets the faithful apart for a special holy life and purpose.

SEVENTH-DAY ADVENTISTS

Several movements within the churches in the early 1800s looked for the Advent, or the return or second coming of Christ, in the near future. William Miller, of Low Hampton, New York, a Baptist, led a movement expecting Christ to return in 1844. Out of this group, and others who differed with the "Millerites," came the Adventist movement. The Seventh-day Adventists are so-called because of a preference for keeping the original Sabbath on Saturday instead of Sunday as a day of rest.

A principal leader was Ellen Harmon (later Mrs. James White). A former Methodist, she saw a number of visions and became author of books on the life and teachings of Jesus and other religious subjects.

Baptism by immersion and the Lord's Supper are "outward" signs of God working within a person. Adventists also practice foot-washing as a rite of humility. Top leadership rests in an executive committee named by a general conference that meets every five years.

A young Seventh-day Adventist, Russell Chin, fifteen, of Keene, Texas, became a member at age eleven, when he was baptized after attending a series of classes. A talented violin and piano player, Russell often plays for the church. He thinks emphasizing Sabbath observance is an important part of his faith. "Sabbath is such a time of peace and rest from the pressures of the week," he says. "I think it is God's way of making life bearable until Jesus comes."

SWEDENBORGIANS

CHURCHES OF THE NEW JERUSALEM

The Swedish scientist and member of parliament, Emmanuel Swedenborg, had a series of dreams and visions. In some of them he talked with members of the spirit world. He reported witnessing a part of the Last Judgment and told of the coming of a New Jerusalem, or the "Descent of the Holy City."

Swedenborgians do not believe in the Trinity as such, but that the Trinity exists in Jesus, whom they regard as God. Besides the Bible, Swedenborgians also look to thirty volumes by Swedenborg on the inner or spiritual meaning of the Bible.

NITARIAN UNIVERSALIST ASSOCIATION

It is perhaps easier to say what Unitarian Universalists do not believe than to say what they believe, beyond saying they believe in God. They do not believe in the Trinity: Jesus is human. In fact, a statement of the church says no person or congregation "shall be required to subscribe to any particular interpretation of religion, or to any particular religious belief or creed." Members generally do not believe in heaven or hell. There are also no sacraments. Emphasis in many sermons are on the principles that work in life, such as love. Membership in some of the churches consists of being eighteen and signing a membership book.

The church is a merger of the American Unitarian Association and the Universalist Church of America that took place in 1961. Historically, the Association draws on the teachings of three men of the sixteenth century: Lelio and Fausto Sozzini, who were Italian anti-Trinitarians, and Jacobus Arminius, who believed salvation was open to all and not just to those who are chosen or predestined.

NITED CHURCH OF CHRIST

A number of traditions or backgrounds are blended in the United Church of Christ. A rather new body, it was formed in 1957 from a merger of the Congregational Christian Churches and the Evangelical and Reformed Church. Each of these previous churches had represented church bodies of diverse background. The United Church of Christ has a congregational type of government in that each local church is its own authority.

There are two sacraments—baptism, usually of infants, and the Lord's Supper. There is also a confirmation rite, usually at age thirteen or fourteen.

Top authority of the United Church of Christ rests in a General Synod of lay and clergy delegates which meets every two years. The church has powerful boards and agencies that do much of the work of the church.

APPENDIX: ADDRESSES OF GROUPS

If you wish more information about religions and groups in this book, these places might be able to help you.

THE JEWISH PATH

American Jewish Committee
165 E. 56th St.
New York, NY 10022

American Jewish Congress
15 E. 84th St.
New York, NY 10028

Synagogue Council of America
327 Lexington Ave.
New York, NY 10016

American Jewish Historical Society
2 Thornton Rd.
Waltham, MA 02154

THE HINDU PATH

Vedanta Society of Northern California
2323 Vallejo St.
San Francisco, CA 94123

Hindu Temple
25 E. Taunton Ave.
Berlin, NJ 08009

Palani Swami Temple and
   Hinduism Today
3575 Sacramento St.
San Francisco, CA 94118

Gandhi Memorial Center
4748 Western Ave.
Bethesda, MD 20816

THE BUDDHIST PATH

Buddhist Vihara Society, Inc.
Washington Buddhist Vihara
5017 Sixteenth St., N.W.
Washington, DC 20001

Buddhist Association of America
109 Waverly Place
San Francisco, CA 94108

The Vajradhatu Sun
(Bimonthly newspaper)
1345 Spruce St.
Boulder, CO 80302

Naropa Institute
2130 Arapahoe Ave.
Boulder, CO 80302

Buddha Dhamma Research Society Inc.
2033 W. 7th
Los Angeles, CA 90057

International Buddhist Meditation
   Center
928 W. New Hampshire Ave.
Los Angeles, CA 90004

Zen Buddhist Center of Washington, D.C.
   Inc.
7004 9th St., N.W.
Washington, DC 20012

THE ISLAMIC PATH

Federation of Islamic Associations in the
  United States and Canada
300 E. 44th St.
New York, NY 10017

Islamic Center of San Francisco
400 Crescent Ave.
San Francisco, CA 94110

United Moslems of America
1564 Market St.
San Francisco, CA 94102

World Community Al-Islam in the West
7351 S. Stony Island Ave.
Chicago, IL 60649

The Islamic Center of America
15571 Joy Road
Detroit, MI 48228

The Islamic Center
2551 Massachusetts Ave., N.W.
Washington, D.C. 20008

Islamic Items
(Independent Newsletter on Modern
  Islamic Thought)
1500 Massachusetts Ave. N.W.
Washington, DC 20005

THE CHRISTIAN PATH

Roman Catholics
National Conference of Catholic Bishops
1312 Massachusetts Ave., N.W.
Washington, DC 20005

National Council of Catholic Laity
P.O. Box 14525
Cincinnati, OH 45214

National Catholic Educational
  Association
1077 30th St. N.W., Suite 100
Washington, DC 20007

Greek Orthodox
Greek Orthodox Archdiocese of North
  and South America
8–10 E. 79th St.
New York, NY 10021

Episcopalians
The Episcopal Church
Episcopal Church Center
815 Second Ave.
New York, NY 10017

Lutherans
Lutheran Council in the U.S.A.
360 Park Ave. So.
New York, NY 10010

Presbyterians
Office of the General Assembly
Presbyterian Church (U.S.A.)
475 Riverside Dr., Room 1201
New York, NY 10115

Methodists
General Commission on
  Communication
United Methodist Church
810 12th Ave. S.
Nashville, TN 37203

Department of Christian Education
African Methodist Episcopal Church
500 8th Ave. S.
Nashville, TN 37203

Department of Christian Education
A.M.E. Zion Church
128 E. 58th St.
Chicago, IL 60637

Baptists
Board of National Ministries
American Baptist Churches in the U.S.A.
Valley Forge, PA 19481

Education Commission
Southern Baptist Convention
901 Commerce St.
Nashville, TN 37203

Education Board
National Baptist Convention of America
3538 Jackson Ave.
New Orleans, LA 70113

Education Board
National Baptist Convention, U.S.A.
903 Looney St.
Memphis, TN 38107

Pentecostals
Division of Communications
Assemblies of God
1445 Boonville Ave.
Springfield, MO 65802

Adventists
Communication Department
Seventh-day Adventists
6840 Eastern Ave. N.W.
Washington, DC 20012

Amish
Old Order Amish Church
Raber's Book Store
Baltic, OH 43804

Armenian Apostolic
Diocese of the Armenian
    Church of America
630 Second Ave.
New York, NY 10016

Baha'i Faith
National Spiritual Assembly
536 Sheridan Rd.
Wilmette, IL 60091

Brethren
Church of the Brethren
1451 Dundee Ave.
Elgin, IL 60120

Christian and Missionary Alliance
Division of Church Ministries
The Christian and Missionary Alliance
350 N. Highland Ave.
Nyack, NY 10960

Christian Science
Church of Christ, Scientist
Christian Science Church Center
Boston, MA 02115

Church of God
Church of God (Anderson, Ind.)
Executive Council
Box 2420
Anderson, IN 46018

Church of God in Christ
Office of the General Secretary
Church of God in Christ
272 S. Main St.
Memphis, TN 38103

Coptics
Coptic Orthodox Church
427 East Side Ave.
Jersey City, NY 07304

Disciples
General Assembly Office
Christian Church (Disciples of Christ)
222 S. Downey Ave., Box 1986
Indianapolis, IN 46206

Jehovah's Witnesses
Jehovah's Witnesses
25 Columbia Heights
Brooklyn, NY 11201

Mennonites
Mennonite Church
528 E. Madison St.
Lombard, IL 60148

Moravians
Moravian Church in America
1021 Center St.
Bethlehem, PA 18016

Mormons
Church of Jesus Christ of Latter-day
    Saints
30 East North Temple St.
Salt Lake City, UT 84150

Nazarenes
Church of the Nazarene
6401 The Paseo
Kansas City, MO 64131

Quakers
Friends United Meeting
101 Quaker Hill Dr.
Richmond, IN 47374

Friends General Conference
1520-B Race St.
Philadelphia, PA 19102

Reformed Church in America
Office of Promotion, Communications
    and Development
Reformed Church in America
475 Riverside Dr.
New York, NY 10115

Salvation Army
National Commander
Salvation Army
799 Bloomfield Ave.
Verona, NJ 07044

Swedenborgians (Church of the
  New Jerusalem)
General Convention,
  The Swedenborgian Church
The Messenger Magazine
48 Sargent St.
Newton, MA 02158

Unitarian Universalist Association
Executive Vice President
Unitarian Universalist Association
25 Beacon St.
Boston, MA 02108

United Church of Christ
Secretary, United Church of Christ
105 Madison Ave.
New York, NY 10016

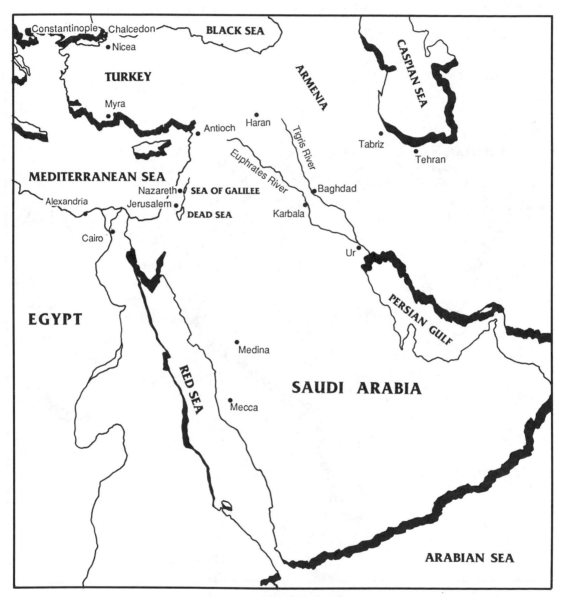

The Seedbed of Judaism and Islam

173

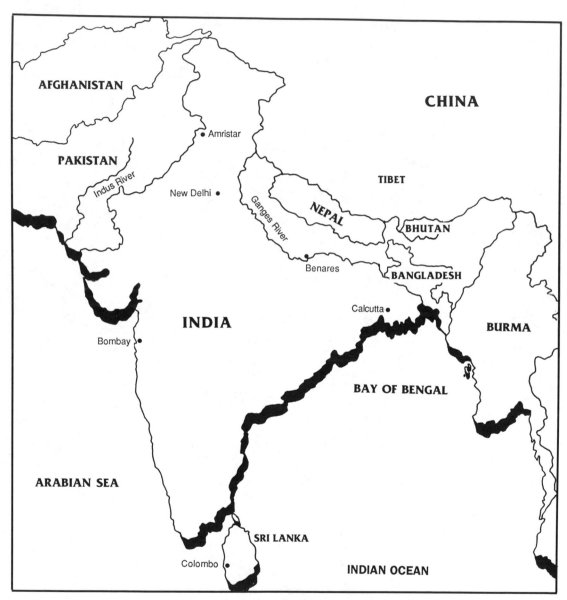

The Cradle of Hinduism and Buddhism

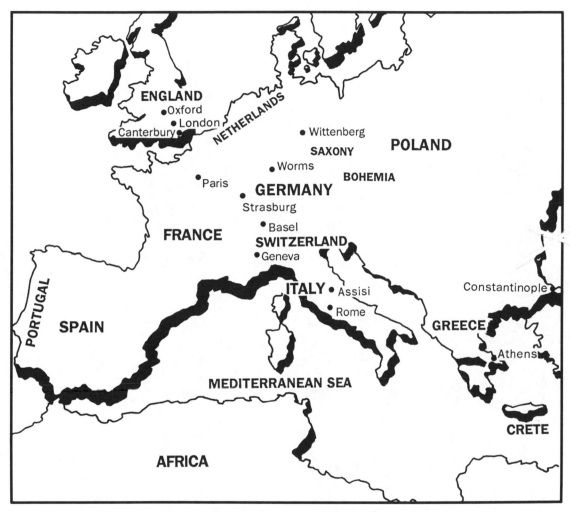

Key Places in the History of Christianity

INDEX

ABOUT THE AUTHOR

HILEY H. WARD teaches journalism at Temple University in Philadelphia and edits *Media History Digest*, published by *Editor & Publisher*, New York. For fourteen years, he was religion editor of the *Detroit Free Press*.

Winner of many awards for his religion writing and reporting, Professor Ward has also contributed articles to major publications, including *Newsday*, the *Chicago Tribune*, *USA Today*, and the *Washington Post*. He is currently film columnist for *National Christian Reporter* and other periodicals.

Among the fourteen published books by this writer are: *Creative Giving, Space-Age Sunday, Ecumania, Rock 2000, Feeling Good About Myself* (for and about teenagers), and *Professional Newswriting*.

After attending public schools, Hiley Ward went to William Jewell College in Missouri for his B.A., and Berkeley Baptist Divinity School in California for an M.A. degree. Then he received his Master of Divinity degree from McCormick Theological Seminary, Chicago, and took a Ph.D. in journalism history and international communication at the University of Minnesota.

Now living in Warrington, Pennsylvania, near Philadelphia, with his wife, Joan Bastel, who is a newspaper editor, Dr. Ward has traveled extensively in Europe and the Middle East. The editing-writing couple have four cats, two dogs and one rabbit.